GROWN UP KIDS

A PARENT'S GUIDE TO ADULT RELATIONSHIPS

SHIRLEY COOK

All Scripture references are from the *Holy Bible, New International Version*. Copyright © 1973, 1978, 1984 International Bible Society. Used by permission of Zondervan Bible Publishers.

Accent Books™ is an imprint of David C. Cook Publishing Co.
David C. Cook Publishing Co., Elgin, Illinois 60120
David C. Cook Publishing Co., Weston, Ontario
Nova Distribution Ltd., Newton Abbot, England

GROWN UP KIDS
©1987 by Shirley Cook

Cover design by Graphically Speaking, Inc.
First Printing, 1987
Printed in the United States of America
96 95 94 93 92 6 5 4 3 2

Library of Congress Catalog Card Number 86-72369
ISBN 0-78140-526-2

*Dedicated To
My Grown-Up Kids:
Greg, Kathy, Dan, Christy,
Becky, and Barby*

CONTENTS

Introduction

O UR FAMILY, ALONG with several others, sat around the smoke filled room listening to the counselor. "Chemical dependency affects the whole family," she said. "For every addict, six people are intimately involved—sometimes without even realizing that their loved one is addicted."

I glanced across the room to our tall, dark and handsome son, a self-admitted participant in an alcohol abuse program. My thoughts went back twenty-nine years before when I first held him in my arms. Our third child. How special! Always alert, bright and full of mischief, this son had the potential to go wherever and be whatever he wanted.

His eyes met mine, and though he knew we, as his family, were suffering with him, he also knew we were proud of his decision to enter the hospital for the month-long treatment. And we were all praying—really praying.

My eyes drifted to our other grown-up kids. Two had begun marriages which ended in divorce and through the experience had grown in patience and compassion. One had survived the hippie movement with its drugs and drop-out philosophy and was now happily married, living a productive life. Another had just completed six years of college, was married and expecting a baby in several months. Our oldest daughter, a single woman, had recently been informed that her job had been phased out, and so far every interview and been a dead end. The youngest, an eighteen-year-old who still lived at home, reached for her dad's hand as she openly shared her love and concern for her brother.

One by one, each person in the room was encouraged to voice the fears and feelings they had about their loved one in the program. As I listened, I realized for the first time that the hardest years of family life are not those late-night feedings, bouts with childhood diseases, and unfinished homework. The really heavy stuff begins with our grown-up kids, and how we each meet those challenges depends a great deal on the relationships and bonding that have gone before.

But no matter what has gone before, there is no reason to despair. Even if our expectations have been shattered and to salvage the remaining pieces seems impossible, there is still hope. We can repair, rebuild, and begin to enjoy loving kinship as a family. God's

Word gives us this assurance in Hebrews 3:4, 6b; "For every house is built by someone, but God is the builder of everything. . . . And we are his house, if we hold on to our courage and the hope of which we boast." Then Hebrews 6:1 adds, "Therefore let us . . . go on to maturity . . ."

God, courage and hope. Leading us on to maturity. As we look honestly at our families, and especially at ourselves, let us be willing, as parents, to accept responsibility for our lives and to trust our grown-up kids to do the same. It takes a lot of love and maybe even a miracle, but God is good at both.

"An obstinate man does not hold opinions, but they hold him."—Plato

1

Square One

REMEMBER THE DAY YOU recited vows that changed your status from "single" to "couple"? You were starting out on an adventure with the one you loved, and for those first months, and possibly years, just the two of you shared the bedroom, the bathroom and the breakfast table. This was an important time in your lives when you were setting goals, getting to know each other better, and just growing as individuals.

Then along came the first baby. What hopes for the future! You would be the best parents in the whole wide world. And you tried.

If it was your goal and commitment to have a family that glorified God, you set out with a spirit of awe linked with strong spiritual convictions. If you began your family life without God in the center, your task was formidable, but you pressed on, determined to give your child the best nurturing you could. Then brothers and sisters began to arrive. (In our family, the final count was six. I've often said that God gives us children to help us learn His lessons, and if I hadn't been such a slow learner, He'd probably have given me only two.)

The years that follow the birth of that first child are the training, loving, teaching years, and though it's the parents' job to implement these tasks, I've noticed that in some families, the children take over. In others, the parents grow so dependent on the role of total provision that they refuse to let go.

But after those eighteen or so years, the time comes to release our now grown-up kids. To be honest, this has always been hard for me to do. Friends have said, "I imagine each time a child grows up and leaves home, it gets a little easier, doesn't it?" I'm not sure that it's easier—just different.

When the first child left home, he was only eighteen, and his leaving was sad because, though he still lived in our city, he had embraced the hippie way of life and I was concerned for him. The next, a daughter, went to a university about forty miles away, and I felt more relaxed knowing she lived in a women's dorm. When the next son moved out, he moved into an apartment with a friend from church. Though he seldom came by, I thought he was doing well. Our fourth child left home on her wedding day, and because she was only eighteen, I had fears that she would have a difficult time. The fifth, a daughter, moved to San Francisco to take an apartment with two girlfriends while she attended university there. I admit to imagining all kinds of worrisome things before truly releasing her.

Now there is only one child left at home, and soon she will be moving four hundred miles away to attend college in Southern California. But I've already worked to consciously release her. In fact, I recorded this event in my journal the month after she graduated from high school.

Lord, this morning, I give my daughter back to you. Thank you for the great joy she has brought to me as a mother. Thank you for allowing us this beautiful and priceless treasure for eighteen years—years that have given me a great purpose in my life. But now she is totally yours. She's ready. She's ready for the testing of those strengths you have been building into her life. She's completed her required education and passed with flying colors.

She's completed the groundwork in human relations at home and succeeded in every detail. She's learned discipline in her commitment to you and your Word and is learning daily to apply it to her life. She's learning to know her own body, her own soul, and her own spirit. These are lessons some people never learn.

I know you have great plans for her life, and I don't want to interfere or interject my will and perhaps get her off the direction you want to lead her. So Lord, this is it. Time to give back this treasure and trust you to keep and use her as you will.

Several days after writing this, I let my daughter read it. We both cried, yet they were good tears. Tears of release and relinquishment. Tears of freedom. Every now and then I have to remind myself that I have let go, especially if I see her taking a path I would not choose. But God has promised to guide our children and complete the good work He has begun. And I believe it.

When that last now grown-up kid leaves, my husband and I will be back where we began. It will once again be just the two of us. We've been preparing for those years by sharing our pleasures and pains and also by developing individual and personal interests. Yet I know from observation and also from the stories friends tell me that these latter years of "Just We Two" will not always be just that. There will be grown-up kids with their spouses and children whose disappointments and problems we'll be sharing. We'll share their joys, too.

How we as parents can adjust to the relationships of the extended family is the purpose of this book, and although there are no "pat" answers, we can find guidance, strength and hope in the Word of God as our ultimate authority and in the case histories of others who have already trod this path.

The foundation of this book, of our lives, and of our relationships is the Word of God. We can count on its precepts to take us all the way from "Square One" to the finish line. No matter how difficult—or easy—the way becomes, remember, "The Lord will guide you always, he will satisfy your needs in a sun-scorched land and will strengthen your frame" (Isaiah 58:11).

GET READY

As I write this, I see some readers glancing at the title, then putting the book down because their children are still in elementary or junior high school. But my prayer is that you will pick it up again and take it home. I remember hearing, "When your children start opening the door by themselves, before you know it, they're grown." That was true. It happened. My kids—all six of them—are grown now, and I'm glad I got ready. Are you getting ready for that time? What does it involve? Why do parents need to prepare for it?

The process of letting go begins as soon as our kids begin to make decisions of their own—from the toys they want to play with, to the friends they want to share with, to the clothes they want to wear. We can marvel at their growth and change, encourage it, and pursue open discussions of right and wrong, values and ethics, or we can fight it. We can demand strict, unquestioning adherence to our way of doing things and cripple that growth. Parents need to decide their weak points and places of vulnerability so that they enter the arena of adult relationships honestly. Why? Because it involves a whole new relationship. Of course, we'll always be parent and child, but even more that that, as adults we can be friends! We are no longer responsible for seeing that our son washes behind his ears or picks up his clothes. We hope he learned that before he was grown. Neither do we have to remind our daughters to pay their bills or to comb their hair. As mature women they are accountable for their own actions—and the consequences. Hopefully, by the time they reach eighteen, they've already been well-tutored in "choices and consequences."

If our grown children didn't learn personal dependability before leaving home, it's not too late for them to learn, but it is too late for us to teach them. Interfering in an adult child's life can only lead to misunderstandings and estrangements. Our place in the lives of our adult children is as equals. Now we can share our likes and dislikes and respect our differences. It's not only okay, it can even be fun! Many parents and children relish the changes and enjoy the process of learning and teaching each other new things, new ideas, new ways of communication.

Of course, this is the ideal: that our children have matured and that we have, too. Unfortunately, that is not always the case. In some instances, parents slip back into childish ways, moping and complaining that they're neglected. Their children either fight back by staying away or they assume a martyr attitude that says, "I have to go see the folks twice a week—or else!"

Knowing the possibilities of misunderstanding and estrangement that can occur, we can use the years before our children grow up to get ready—to prepare ourselves to be interesting, growing mature friends. We can choose to be open to growth and willing to accept our children's adulthood.

GET SET

Learning to communicate with our children while they are young prepares the way to an open exchange of feelings when they're grown. This includes being willing to admit when we're wrong, and even asking our child's forgiveness when necessary. Parents with this balance in their lives show by example how to truly love—and isn't that what families are all about?

The other day one of my sons came to me with the words, "Mom, I'm sorry that I was so adamant in expressing my feelings about the government yesterday."

"But you have a right to your own opinions," I said.

"I know, but I didn't have to be so loud about it."

After he left, I thought back to the countless arguments (discussions!) we had during his teenage years. He was so sure he was right, and I was so sure I was. Then I remembered going to his room one night after he'd gone to bed. I apologized for trying to make him believe as I did, and he had been quick to accept my apology. We were learning to communicate in those days, and today those doors are still open. We are good friends, willing to grant each other the right to our own opinions without feeling threatened by the differences.

That kind of openness takes a lifetime to learn, especially when we're wrong and somehow believe it is demeaning to admit it. I had to relearn this lesson only recently when one of my daughters asked my opinion of her new friend.

"Oh, I didn't care much for him," I said without thinking.

The hurt expression on her face showed I had been tactless. But she'd asked, hadn't she? I didn't want to lie.

After she left, I knew I had to ask her forgiveness. Even though I had spoken the truth, it had been in a harsh manner. I had hurt my daughter, and it was up to me to make things right. It wasn't easy, but it was healing. She forgave my bluntness, and I'm learning to think before I speak.

Go

Okay. It sounds wonderful, you say, but I haven't seen any courses offered on "Developing Adult Parent-Child Relationships 101. "Where can I get the wisdom needed to become a parent/friend? If most of my life has slipped by and I've not prepared for this stage, what can I do? If my kids are not only ruining their lives—at least in my opinion—but my peace of mind as well, how can I gain the serenity to face each day?

An old prayer has made a fresh impact on me these past few months.

"Lord, grant me the Serenity to accept the things I cannot change; Courage to change the things I can; and Wisdom to know the difference."

The Lord is our answer. Whatever we need, He will supply. Do I need patience? You bet! Do I need love? Sure do! Do I need joy? Uh huh!

How do I get all of that? "The fruit of the Spirit is love, joy, peace, patience, kindness, goodness, faithfulness, gentleness and self-control" (Galatians 5:22-23).

All that?

All that and more.

God, through the working of His Holy Spirit, is everything we need now—if our children are small, are teenagers, or are these people we call our grown-up kids.

And He is waiting for you and me to believe it. Each day requires a new commitment to release our adult children to Him, a new determination to work on our attitudes, and a new enjoyment of the challenges these exciting new friends present.

FOR DISCUSSION AND ENCOURAGEMENT

- Think back. What goals did you have as parents when you welcomed that first child into your family? Have you been able to fulfill any or all of them? Talk this over with your children. Get their ideas on what makes a successful family.

- If your children are small, discuss how you might get ready for their adult years. If they are grown-up, discuss how you can build stronger friendships with them.

- How did you feel when your children moved from the family home? How did you feel when you left your parents' home? Discuss this with your kids. You may want to find out how your parents felt when you grew up.

- In what ways does a personal relationship with Christ affect the development of family members? Find some biblical examples of families who left God out of their lives. Find some who built their homes according to God's plan.

- Define serenity. What are some things in your family that you cannot change? Some things you can change? Do you know the difference?

- Read Proverbs 1:8-19, and apply it to your family situation.

"When you expect the best, you release a magnetic force in your mind which by a law of attraction tends to bring the best to you."

—William James

2

Accentuate the Positive

THIS BOOK ADDRESSES some of the challenges and choices involved in relating with our grown-up kids and can encourage each of us. But before I go on with possible problems and pitfalls, I want to take a long, loving look at the joys our adult children bring.

I not only love my kids, I really like them. Each of the six are so different that it's fun to be with them and get to know them.

Get to know them?

"Surely," you must be saying out of the corner of your mouth, "if you don't know them by the time they're grown, your elevator must have stalled before reaching the top floor."

No. Not really. These grown-up kids are still growing, and so are their parents. As we grow, we change opinions, we develop new interests, and we slowly become well-rounded persons. As we progress, it is necessary to be open to one another and get to know—really know—what's going on in our heads. If you think about it, that may be one reason parents and adult children have problems relating. We fail to stay current with each other.

Around the time our children near their twenties, we begin to take each other for granted. We don't allow them any more personal growth, and neither do they give us that right. (But Mom and Dad have never changed!) But when we do that, we form conclusions and judgments based on the past instead of the present.

I was surprised when the daughter who has always passively accepted my suggestions suddenly flared when I said, "Why don't you buy the pink sweater, instead of that red one? You look better in pink."

Not only has her taste in color changed in the past year, but she has a new awareness of who she is. No longer unsure of herself, she is becoming assertive and confident . . . a little confusing to me, but a lot more fun! She thinks I'm more fun, too. I'm not as rigid and unbending as I was a few years ago. My interests have broadened to include some new ideas.

It's always a good idea to focus on the joys and blessing our children bring—especially if we're going through a "climbing the wall" period with one of them. It may take some creative thinking, but why not give it a try? Psychologists and medical doctors have proven that happy thoughts and a humorous outlook can relieve many stress-related illnesses . . . something God's Word told us long ago.

A cheerful heart is good medicine, but a crushed spirit dries up the bones. (Proverbs 17:22)

Pleasant words are a honeycomb, sweet to the soul and healing to the bones. (Proverbs 16:24)

happy heart makes the face cheerful, but heartache crushes the spirit. . . . A man finds joy in giving an apt reply—and how good is a timely word! Proverbs 15:13,23)

ACCENTUATE THE POSITIVE

You may rue the day your growing-up kid learned to drive, but try to remember what it was like before: into the car, off to the dentist; back in the car, a stop at the soccer field; into the car again for a trip to the grocery store; and then another visit to the gas pumps. At least now you can remove the revolving doors from your suburban taxicab and send the kids off to do their own errands. They'll probably even be glad to do some of yours. Be happy you don't have to do all the driving. There—a joy—a blessing, and it wasn't too hard to find.

How about another? If you sons and daughters are still at home and they're over thirty-years-old, remember back to the days when you wondered where they were. Now you know. Well, you may consider that a mixed blessing, but at least the corners of your mouth are turning up a little.

Grown-up kids can help us see ourselves as we really are. They're often more honest than we appreciate, but if we listen, we will not only improve our relationship with our children, but we can also improve ourselves. Perhaps another mixed blessing, but also a potentially fascinating "mirror."

I've also gained some of my greatest spiritual insights from my adult children. They sometimes take the loftiest truths and without trying, translate them into present-day living.

For instance, the other day the son who is recovering from alcoholism dropped by. We've become close these past months, and I've felt especially happy that he likes to share his life with me now. I always try to be "up" when he comes so I can be an encouragement, but he caught me on a "down" day. after several minutes, I apologized for my mood.

"I don't expect you to always be happy, Mom," he said. "No one is happy all the time. If we didn't have some bad days, how could we appreciate the good ones?"

Smack! "Shall we accept good from God, and not trouble?" (Job 2:10). Another truth from God's Word hit me—brought home by my son. He's learning to be honest about his feelings and to accept them. I want to learn this, too.

On the subject of acceptance, I've come across the best little pamphlet entitled just that, "Acceptance." It's written by Vincent P. Collins. If you can get a copy, I think you'll find it a treasure, too. In twenty-three short pages, he covers our worries about the future: other people's problems and how we try to solve them, hurt feelings, divine providence, and what it means to be contented—serene. Its message is so pertinent and helpful that I read it almost every day.

Yes, we need to accentuate the positive in the lives of our children. In doing so, we'll learn to accept them and ourselves as we are and learn more of the depths of what love really is. And love, sometimes a tough love, must be the central force in our lives if we want to solve the problems we face as parents of grown-up kids.

My friend Alice brought this home to me one day. She says she loves her daughter, and I'm sure she does, but the way she expresses her love is destroying their respect for each other. There are a lot of positive things in their relationship. They enjoy going places together, and they spend hours talking and laughing. But Alice is beginning to confuse love with her need to be needed. And her daughter, instead of growing toward independence, has developed a dependency that borders on parasitism—for both of them.

The daughter, twenty-two-year-old Toni, wrecked the car her mother paid for, ran up credit cards her mother paid off, and let her boyfriend gamble away her savings account. Now she has returned home to live with mom and dad because she quit her job, and she doesn't want to live with her boyfriend anymore.

Alice is beside herself. Her nerves are shot. She takes tranquilizers to get through the day and dreads going home from work each night. "But I just love her too much to tell her to leave," she says.

Yes, Alice does love Toni. Toni is, after all, her only child, but Toni is a grown-up child. This mother needs to examine her love to see if her actions are actually the result of her own need to be loved rather than concern for her daughter.

Hard words, aren't they? But they are true ones. Positive ones.

If Alice enjoyed having her daughter with her, that might be a different story, but she's unhappy. She feels guilty for her suppressed feelings, and Toni suffers the same guilt and unhappiness. She admits she has lost respect for her mother, and asks, "Why does she let people use her?" Yet she doesn't admit to being among the users.

I'm not sure how I would react in the same situation. I know what I might tell Alice to do, but could I do it myself?

This past summer our son and his wife moved into our house with everything they own minus their furniture. They had made long-range plans to quit their jobs in another state; move their sailboat and themselves to California; and from here, begin a two year "retirement." When they arrived, we were ready for them. They only needed a couple of weeks to get their boat ready. Then they would use the past four years' savings to live on while they made trips to Mexico and possibly Hawaii.

These are intelligent, thoughtful adults who know what they want, plan well in advance, and go for it. The entire family supported them in this exciting endeavor. And I am among their chief supporters. But. . . .

The two weeks became two months. We gave up our bedroom and bedded down in the den where we could be close to our books, our closets, and our bathroom. But my back began to long for its accustomed mattress. I had to avert my eyes when I passed my bedroom loaded down with stacks of their books, bags of clothes, suitcases, and boxes. Even the garage, which is already overflowing with our own mess, bulged with boat equipment, more bags of clothes, and bigger boxes.

Our grown-up kids tried to ease the burden by helping with the cooking and yard work. They even periodically assured us, "It won't be long now. We're sorry to have to stay here for such a long time."

I admit to getting anxious sometimes. I love my privacy and the peace and quiet I've earned after raising six children in a medium-sized house. But knowing that in September they would be on their boat, heading toward Mexico, helped me through the days when I felt frustrated and closed in. However, I wonder how I would have handled the situation if they had had no plans to move on?

I love these two. However, I wouldn't want them to live with me indefinitely. Neither would they want to live with us on a permanent basis. But suppose they decided it would be a good idea to wait indefinitely before leaving? What then? As parents, would we be unloving or lack understanding if we asked them to get an apartment for those next few months? Not if that's what we really wanted . . . and if felt it necessary in order to maintain our positive feelings for each other. Our relationship is that important to us.

Parents do neither children nor themselves good by swallowing their true feelings while the blood pressure rises. We only become resentful and begin to live a lie. We want—and need—to take positive steps to affirm the good qualities we see in our children, but then we must courageously speak the truth. How do you accomplish that peacefully? An Arab proverb says, "When you shoot an arrow of truth, dip its point in honey."

As those hot days dragged by, I had to face my own feelings, and I also had the opportunity to accentuate the positive. But I had to choose that option over the other choice of looking only at the negatives.

I learned some lessons while our adult children lived with us that I wouldn't have otherwise. As a young married couple, they are totally devoted to one another. They work together as a unit whether they're constructing a boat or a pizza. In the two months we were under each other's noses, I never heard them use sharp or sarcastic words to each other or to us. Their voices were soft and gentle; their manner quiet and easygoing.

Oh, if only some of that would rub off on me!

We had leisurely early morning talks before beginning the day, and we reached the end of the day with more of the same. We laughed and joked throughout the inconvenience and the excitement of their projected trip. What a joy this past summer has been! My number one son, who at one period in his life gave me great concern, has come back to bless me. I thought I knew him, but now I know him better. I like him, respect him, and look forward to his return from that voyage. I hope they stay with us for at least two more months!

Throughout life we can expect problems, detours and uphill climbs, but that's how we grow. As we face trials and work through them, our spirits are fashioned in the design God has planned for our lives. God has promised that in His Word. Need encouragement? Read Jeremiah 29:11-13, Romans 8:28-29, and Romans 12:1-2.

Turning our heads and denying a problem, like Alice is doing, only magnifies it. Neither Alice nor Toni will grow until they solve their mutual problem. For Alice, it means she must be honest with her daughter. She has to tell her how unhappy she is and ask her to step out on her own, get a job, and find an apartment. And Toni must let go of her infantile dependence on her mother.

This will cause them to love each other more, not less. They will respect each other again, and they'll both learn independence—the true independence that allows one to trust in God rather than men.

A good guide to this difficult situation?

Get rid of all bitterness, rage and anger, brawling and slander, along with every form of malice. Be kind and compassionate to one another, forgiving each other, just as in Christ God forgave you. (Ephesians 4:31-32)

FOR DISCUSSION AND ENCOURAGEMENT

- Make a list of five positive attributes you see in each of your children. Over the next week, share the items on the list with each child. If a grown-up child lives far away, write a letter to express one of the characteristics you appreciate.

- Make a list of five positive attributes you see in your own life. Perhaps you've not had the proper perspective concerning your own value. For the next five days, ask God to help you strengthen those positive characteristics. Let them reflect and shine in your home.

- Do you want a closer relationship with your child? You can begin by deepening your relationship with the Lord.

  1. Confess your failures and fears. (Romans 10:9-10 and Hebrews 4:15-16)

  2. Ask Jesus Christ to forgive and cleans you. (I John 1:9)

  3. Be willing to make restitution where necessary. (Luke 19:8, Matthew 18:21-22)

- Overcome your fear of rejection and misunderstanding by courageously sharing your true feelings with your adult child. The risk is worth it!

- Read the entire fourth chapter of Ephesians, replacing the word "you" with your own name. This exercise will take time—but everything worthwhile does.

Instead, speaking the truth in love, we will in all things grow up into him who is the Head, that is, Christ. From him the whole body, joined and held together by every supporting ligament, grows and builds itself up in love, as each part does its work. —Ephesians 4:15-16

3

Kid Games

Sara rushed into the sanctuary and sat down beside me, clutching the bulletin tightly in one hand. After several minutes, this tall, lovely blonde opened her Bible, breathed a deep sigh and began to relax. As we waited for the service to begin, she leaned toward me and whispered, "Things are pretty rough at home." A waft of perfume lingered as she straightened herself.

I wasn't sure what she meant, but I knew from past conversations that her grown-up kids were a constant source of concern. I prayed for her as the pastor expounded on patience, and when we finally stood to leave, she drew me aside.

"You know our twenty-two-year old finally moved out and we thought we could begin enjoying our home—and now our daughter has moved in!" Tears welled in her large blue eyes. "I feel like I'm running around in circles, and she's calling the shots."

> *Ring-around-the-rosies,*
> *A pocket full of posies,*
> *Ashes, ashes, all fall down!*

Another friend, Gloria, has also been drawn into a kids' game called Hide and Seek by her daughter, Patti, who walked out on her husband, took their child, and disappeared. Gloria heard from one source that Patti is living with a man on the outskirts of town, but no one knows for sure. It's hard enough to wonder where her daughter is, but not knowing about the little grandson is almost too much to bear.

Bill and Maggie's son still plays Cowboys and Indians. He leaves home only long enough to get in debt. Then when the chase gets too hot, he runs back home for mom and dad to provide room and board. They can't get ahead because this hundred-eighty-pound child loves to spend most of his time in the "cookhouse."

When Jack retired, June looked forward to the period of their lives when they could travel, spend mornings lingering over coffee, and just enjoy each other. But Vickie's marriage broke up, and she had to go back to work. They are proud that their daughter is able to support herself and three small children, but. . . .

"Just until I can find a good babysitter, Mom. Honest. I've got an ad in the paper and have talked to lots of people, but you wouldn't want me to trust your grandchildren with just anyone. Would you?"

No, June couldn't stand to have those darlings shuffled around or mistreated in any way. She and Jack would just have to postpone their plans a little longer. Just a little longer. You know the game. Let's Pretend. You be the mommy, the daddy, the grandma and the grandpa.

Kids games. Yet these games are not fun. No one wins. When the sun goes down, you don't go in for dinner and forget about the games. This is real stuff. No one's playing anymore. There are too many hurts: broken marriages, loss of work, illness. Whatever happened to the good old days when the young men and women moved out after graduation and supported themselves happily ever after?

Could we of this generation be at fault for the lack of independence we see in some of our kids or their lack of commitment to hearth and home? Why are they so unconcerned about holding down jobs and advancing in their occupations?

Our minister recently preached through the book of James. In the fifth chapter, we were encouraged to be patient, and we learned that through suffering, patience grows. We heard about a man who lost everything during the Great Depression. He told our pastor, "That was the hardest, most difficult period of my life. I sure learned a lot, though. I learned patience and perseverance. I learned what it meant to rise above adversity." Then without batting an eye, the man added, "I've done everything in my power to keep my children from having to go through those afflictions. I've provided them with all they could ever want."

The pastor could hardly believe his ears. He asked the man, "But why have you wanted to keep your children from learning those valuable lessons? Look how you benefited—how you matured."

If we're asking ourselves why our children have not grown up, maybe we need to face reality. We didn't allow it. We provided too much and continue to do so until our grown-up kids are like overgrown birds that were never nudged out of the nest. The only way they've grown is physically. If they have not learned to use their wings, we may need to ask ourselves how we've contributed to that condition.

Let's go back a minute and take another look at Sara and her daughter. Knowing this mother, I believe she would be the first to admit that, like most of us, she tried to shield her child from discomfort. What mother wouldn't? We bring these little ones into the world and are responsible for their well-being. We feed and clothe them. We help them with homework and give them spending money. We may even buy them cars, gasoline and insurance. We put them through college or lay down the money for their first apartment. But now these "little ones" are grown. They can read and write. They can dress themselves. And to our dismay, we find that they can also go into debt, wreck their cars, drink to excess, and have abortions.

Must we continue to be responsible for their actions? Are we accountable for them or to them the rest of their lives? Did we take on an eternal obligation when we heard that baby's first cry?

No.

The dictionary says that to grow is "to increase by a natural process of development or of enlargement."

Plants grow taller through proper nourishment—as do people; dogs grow more responsive through training—and so do we; but only humans grow wiser by applying the knowledge that comes their way. We do our children great harm if we only feed and train them. Part of our duty as parents is to teach them not only to make decisions, but also to accept responsibility for the outcome of those decisions. Only then will our kids grow, as Jesus did, "in wisdom and stature, and in favor with God and men" (Luke 2:52).

But don't get me wrong. Sara is not to blame for her daughter's actions. She may assume the burden of the car loan she co-signed because of her mother-love; she may take on guilt for the anger she feels at being put upon because of her mother-love; she may even sacrifice her own needs to keep her child from having to leave home with no place to go, again because of her mother-love. But she is not to blame. She is only a mother. Her daughter alone is responsible for her life. She is a grown-up kid. An adult. Her mother is not responsible before God or man to provide the needs and wants of a healthy, educated woman.

Let them both grow up and answer for their own deeds. Ring around the Rosies is for kids.

And how about Gloria? Oh, we could all sympathize with her! The anguish she feels. The worry.

Sometimes it eats her up—and sometimes she eats everything in sight to ease the pain. That precious daughter. How cute she was as a toddler in pink ruffles and ponytails. Now Patti lives with any man who will have her. She's overweight, depressed, and devoid of all self-esteem. Is Gloria responsible? No. She may have made some mistakes while Patti was growing up. We all do. She may not have been the perfect mother she wanted to be. Who is? She rakes the past over the coals day and night. If only she had . . . if only. If she doesn't grow up, Gloria will end up with an ulcer and join Patti in the low self-esteem trap.

We cannot allow ourselves to assume the responsibility for our grown-up kids. As long as we do, they will not grow up.

It may sound cold and hard, but for her own health, Gloria must let go of Patti and go on with her life. There is no turning back. The "what-ifs" and "if-onlys" are vapors from the pit to divert our attention from the ever present Lord who waits to bear our burdens and carry our sorrows. It doesn't pay to shoulder the weight of the world. Only Jesus can do that.

> *Come to me, all you who are weary and burdened, and I will give you rest. Take my yoke upon you and learn from me, for I am gentle and humble in heart, and you will find rest for your souls. For my yoke is easy and my burden is light. (Matthew 11:28-30)*

But maybe you are in the same position as Jack and June. You're needed, you hope for just a short time, and have willingly given up your plans in order to help out. That's good. Your Vickie needs you right now, and soon she'll find a reliable babysitter. However, for Jack and June "soon" has now become a year, and there's no change in sight. Should June tell Jack to go on with the vacation plans while she stays at home to raise another family?

Probably not a good idea. This retired couple has looked forward to the enjoyment of their middle years. They trained, nurtured, and educated Vickie. They provided her with a college degree, gave her a big wedding, and helped her begin her roles as wife and mother. Now the little they have put aside for travel dribbles away on high chairs, playpens and new tennis shoes. They grin and bear it, but their relationship with each other is strained, and their love for Vickie and those "sweeties" begins to feel forced. What can they do?

They can quit playing Let's Pretend, make some new rules, and grow up.

"Vickie, we love you and the kids, but we will only be available for one more month. You must find a babysitter by then, because we're going on vacation—just the two of us."

Hard words? Yes, but we learn patience and perseverance through hardship. Remember? "As you know, we consider blessed those who have persevered." (James 5:11a). Those words could be the greatest blessing you ever give your child. She will learn to lean on God instead of you.

When my daughter was going through a

divorce, I thought about her constantly. Was she safe in that apartment? What kind of friends was she seeing? What would become of her? Often I tossed and turned instead of sleeping. Oh, believe it or not, I prayed too, but I thought it only fair to God that I worry as well as pray. After all, I would be taking the easy way out if I gave up my anxiety. Besides, she might think I didn't love her.

Finally, one Sunday night after watching a James Dobson film about parental relationships, I called her. "Honey, I've something to tell you," I said, knowing how hurt she would be. "I've decided not to worry about you any more. Emotionally I've been holding you close to me like a captured butterfly and you've not been free to use your wings. I just want you to know—I'm letting go—and letting God."

I held my breath, expecting her to cry or at least express some kind of dismay. Instead, her voice rang out over the telephone wire, "Thanks, Mom. That really makes me feel good. Like you trust my judgment."

From that moment on, we both began to grow up and, surprising to me, we grew closer than ever before. The game of "Heavy, heavy hangs over thy head," was over. My daughter and I were learning to trust God instead of our own self-defeating ways.

Are you playing games with your grown-up kids? Have they tied you up in knots and left you to struggle in your own indecision? Do you want someone to give you answers, someone to tell you exactly how to handle the situation you're in? No one can do that. You must find your own answer.

Do you want to go on giving in to your kids and feeling less loving toward them day by day? Or do you want to take charge of your life, and give them the responsibility of managing theirs? It's up to you.

"When I was a child, I talked like a child, I thought like a child, I reasoned like a child. When I became a man (mature), I put childish ways behind me" (I Corinthians 13:11).

Or did I? It's not too late.

FOR DISCUSSION AND ENCOURAGEMENT

- Are you caught in any of these games? Try to mentally establish some game rules:

1. Decide who are the players. If you're playing games with your adult children, determine to be on the same side.

2. Be sure everyone knows the rules. Be loving, be kind, and be mature.

3. Set a time limit. It's okay to be "child-like" in your attitudes, but "childishness" should be discarded.

4. Abide by the Judge's decision. Seek God's guidance through a prayerful study of His Word. "For everyone who asks receives; he who seeks finds; and to him who knocks, the door will be opened" (Matthew 7:8).

- In Three Steps Forward Two Steps Back, Charles Swindoll wrote, "What is a sign of maturity? Practicing what you hear." He said it is one thing to grow OLD; another to grow UP. Write down one childish habit you are willing to give up. Don't expect your child to grow up before you do.

- Do you believe that ignoring a problem will make it go away? Think of some examples that support your theory. Can't think of any? Think of ways to face and work through your problems.

- Is love expressed better through self-sacrifice or confrontation? Does it vary by situation? How? Which reaction would best serve your loved one in the long run?

- Read I Corinthians 13 and measure your love reactions. Don't neglect "rejoices with the truth."

"Self-conquest is the greatest of victories."

—*Plato*

4

Support or Control?

Whats the difference? As a mother, this has been one of the hardest lessons for me to learn. How much support (not financial) do I give my grown-up child? And if I support him/her emotionally, does that give me a right to tell my child how to live?

I've struggled with this ever since our first child left home. After all, as a parent (especially a mother), I have been the guide, supporter, "controller" in that child's life since the day of birth. This is not meant to put down the position of the father in the home. It's just the way things worked out. At least at our house.

In the days of yore when we were young parents of small children, my husband went to work and I stayed home to raise the family. In the evening, the thundering herd would run to the door with squeals and laughter to meet their daddy, and he in turn tossed and tumbled with them while I got dinner on the table. But those few minutes and some free week-end hours were the most he spent with these little people. He had a lot of mouths to feed and worked two jobs. I bathed, burped, and bundled them. It was my job to see to it that they brushed their teeth, said "thank you," knelt for nightly prayers, and made their beds.

As they grew, it was to me they usually brought their problems.

"Joey stole all my marbles, and I'm gonna sock him!"

"My teacher hates me and made me stand in the corner."

"Justin kissed me, and it made me feel all butterflies inside!"

I talked to Joey, made an appointment to see the teacher, and studied up on sex education. I wasn't always sure that I had the right answer, but I did the best I could, and my children looked to me as the "almost-always-wise one." Well, you can see, and I'm sure you know what's coming, how hard it is to suddenly fall off your pedestal when the children begin to look to their peers instead of parents as confidantes and advisors. Wow! Those years between adolescence and adulthood were difficult.

Still, my husband and I managed to hold the upper hand.

"As long as your feet are under our table, you behave in a way that is acceptable to us," was the message to sometimes balking teens.

Have you heard that song before? Sometimes it works, sometimes not. You know it is time to wean your child away from your guidance, and yet you feel you're losing something very important in your life. Suddenly you're wrestling with the question, "How much support or control do I give my grown-up child?"

CONTROL

Let's look at this word first. *The Century Dictionary and Cyclopedia* gives, as the third definition, "To exercise control over; hold in restraint or check; subject to authority; direct; regulate; govern; dominate."

That pretty well covers the responsibilities of a parent, doesn't it? You don't let the little darlings carry the cat by the tail or throw their dinner against the wall. You "exercise control" over them until they learn to control their own primitive instincts.

They are "held in restraint" to keep them from hurting themselves or getting lost. When our youngest daughter was little, I took her shopping, pushing her through the department stores in her stroller until she began to crawl out and disappear under the racks of clothes. One time it took me almost half an hour before I discovered her yellow ponytails behind a display of winter coats. It was then I put a harness on her. I received dirty looks from disapproving matrons, but at least I didn't lose my inquisitive toddler.

As a parent you teach your children the joys of

obedience as opposed to the disadvantages of disobedience; you "direct" them in personal hygiene and safety; you "regulate" their diets and bedtimes; you "govern" the periods of homework and TV. You "dominate" their worlds. In other words, you control your child.

But some parents don't. It's too time consuming, too much bother. But without parental control, our children run wild, and as grown-up kids, they have no pattern of self-control.

As Dr. Laurence J. Peter, author of *The Peter Principle,* said "When a mother hasn't enough willpower to discipline her children, she calls her weakness child psychology."

SUPPORT

Back to the dictionary. "Support: To uphold by aid, encouragement, or countenance; keep from shrinking, sinking, failing, or fainting: as, to support the courage or spirits."

Parents are involved in this activity from the moment they hear that first cry. We "uphold" our baby, pat his little back, rock him gently until the wee hours of the morning, and "aid" in every way we can to make our child comfortable and happy. We "encourage" her as she takes her first faltering steps and kerplunks on her diapered, well-padded bottom. We lovingly take the hand of our kindergartner as he "shrinks" from entering the schoolroom; we hold her slippery arms so she won't "sink" when she first ventures out into the shallow end of the swimming pool. (As a non-swimmer, that's as far as I ever got. In no time at all, the kids were holding *my* slippery arms.) We are also there throughout the high school years helping our children wade through the books so they won't "fail," and we're standing alongside so they won't "faint" when they get their ears pierced.

This is what we do physically and emotionally to support our children. Does this privilege end when our children are grown?

We've found that in our family, the support system between parent and child becomes even stronger as the years progress. Neither of us seeks to control the other, and yet we all endeavor to support each other.

There's a world of difference between "holding in restraint" and "upholding." Recognizing that difference and adapting to it will determine the kind of relationship we have with our grown-up kids.

I was the recipient of this kind of support recently as I recovered from a painful attack of diverticulitis. (Sounds impressive, doesn't it?) My oldest daughter, knowing my tendency to ignore my own physical problems, called to see that I made a doctor's appointment. Her words bordered on "control," but I knew she was concerned because she loves me. She didn't hang up until I promised to make an appointment—which I did. Then a few minutes later, I received a bouquet of three pink roses from another daughter with the words, *"Please get well, You need your: ."* In case that baffles you, diverticulitis is an inflammation of the "colon." These grown-up daughters gave me support when I needed it. They are good friends.

Don't get me wrong. This isn't a picture of perfection. We've had to work to get where we are today. They've had trouble with me, and I have had trouble with them. We've had our ups and downs, and because we are human, I'm sure there will be a few more hills to climb as we mature together.

I like the statement by Peter DeVries, a humorist writer: "Who of us is mature enough for offspring before the offspring themselves arrive? The value of marriage is not that adults produce children but that children produce adults."

LET'S GET PRACTICAL

If I as a parent have been controlling my children during their growing up years and am now expected to step aside and offer support only when needed, how can I make this adjustment into maturity?

As a Christian, I need the indwelling power of the Holy Spirit to help me here as in any other endeavor. I don't have the strength in myself to stand back when I see my adult child willfully make wrong choices. I find it hard to keep my mouth shut when he behaves in irresponsible ways. Surely the Lord has given me the "right" to control my child—no matter how old. Hasn't He?

Seeking to answer that question, I checked through my Bible concordance. Surprisingly, though, I found no references to people controlling people. Whenever the word is used in reference to humans, it speaks of self-control. ". . . A wise man keeps himself under control," Proverbs 29:11; ". . . each of you should learn to control his own body, ..." I Thessalonians 4:4. But, to me, this is the best of all: "The mind of sinful man is death; but the mind controlled by the Spirit is life and peace," Romans 8:6. And Galatians 5:22-23 adds, "The fruit of the Spirit is . . . self-control." Perhaps as we parents rely upon God for the self-control needed in our lives, our children will respond by relying on that same strength.

The word self-control comes from a Greek word meaning, "strong, having mastery, able to control one's thoughts and actions." And, it is only as we allow the Holy Spirit to discipline us in self-control that we grow in the ability to exercise it. One thing we never outgrow as parents is the need to be an example to our children. We are their mirrors.

While we are to control ourselves, there are many references to "support" and to "encourage" others in God's Word. It seems to be a godly attribute—one the Lord models for us.

. . . But the Lord was my support. (Psalm 18:18)
. . . Your love, O Lord, supported me. (Psalm 94:18)
. . . But encourage one another daily, ... (Hebrews 3:13)
encourage each other, ... (I Thessalonians 4:18)
Encourage and rebuke with all authority. (Titus 2:15)

And many, many more! Support or control? You decide.

FOR DISCUSSION AND ENCOURAGEMENT

- Are you controlling your child? In what ways? withholding love? pouting? giving too much? Be honest.

- Think of positive ways you can be a support without having to be in control.

- Are your children controlling you? Why? The Holy Spirit offers us the power of self-control. If anything or anyone else is controlling us, we're in trouble.

- To have a good, mature relationship with out adult children makes all those years of training and sacrifice worthwhile. It's worth the effort to support each other.

- Proverbs 2 and 3 are great words from a parent to a child. Read them prayerfully. How can they be applied to your family?

"People are usually more firmly convinced that their opinions are precious than that they are true."—George Santayana

5

Eye-to-Eye

HAVE YOU NOTICED that about the time our children are tall enough for eye-to-eye contact, we also get eye-to-eye conflict? Suddenly we have opposite opinions on "good" music, appropriate dress, friends, religion, and priorities. What happened? Did our children change overnight? Are they only trying to be different? Is it a plot to annoy us? Are they secretly scheming to undermine everything we've taught them—or just cause a few more grey hairs?

Or—have they been weighing our words and actions against their own changing values? Are they fighting an internal struggle to find their own ideals and live them out? Whatever the answer, this period can be one that will bring us closer, eventually, or drive us away from each other. And what a loss that would be!

All children go through this "pulling away" stage at some point and to some degree. It may be so minor that you almost miss it, or it could be so major that you wonder how you'll survive it. Some children don't go through it at eighteen or twenty. They may delay this step until much later in life. For some kids, to disagree with parents can be so threatening to their security that they remain dependent for years—sometimes even into middle age.

A child's rebellion does not necessarily prove he is maturing. Those who fight the hardest to prove a point usually find it most difficult to stand on their own two feet. Those are the ones who may need more love—firm, tough or tender—to encourage their emotional growth.

This works both ways, too. Moms and dads sometimes have a rough time releasing their children. When the disagreements involve issues more serious than preferences in music and clothes, it requires a giant step of faith to commit these loved ones to the Lord and leave their development and growth to Him. There is an old saying with much truth in it that a parent should give a child two priceless gifts—roots and wings.

DESPERATION OR DELIGHT?

Several years ago, I attended a mountain retreat with a gathering of women who were all strangers to me. As I looked at each face and became acquainted through small group studies and large plates of fabulous fare, I thought, "Boy, these gals are sure 'together.'" Their smiles were serene, and even in a mountain setting, their hair stayed in place and their mascara didn't run. I imagined ideal home lives and perfect children. To identify wasn't easy because I was going through some tough times with my family.

Then, the Sunday morning following the last message, the dam broke! Tears began to flow as one after another—wives, mothers, and single women—shared their heartaches and pain.

"I have two sons," began a lovely middle-aged woman. "Many of you know the youngest one. He's a leader of the youth in our church. He's married and we're all looking forward to the birth of their first child." Several minutes passed as she wiped her eyes and took a deep breath. "I just learned," a sob escaped her lips, "I just learned my other son—my firstborn—is a—a homosexual!" The last words were almost whispered, but the room was quiet enough to hear her anguished cry. "What can I do?"

Heads lowered as women reached for tissue. Those nearest stepped to her side and drew her close. Another voice spoke up, "My daughter, my beautiful daughter told me last week that she recently had an abortion—her fourth." This mother, too, spoke through tears. "Each pregnancy was caused by a different man!" She shook her head in disbelief. "I had no idea. I thought she was a little wild—but. . . . ?"

One after another, these lovely daughters of God

confessed the pain in their hearts, pain brought upon them through grown-up children who had once been a source of joy.

Even though the room was heavy with burdens, as we began to pray spontaneously, asking God for wisdom and strength to love and help our children, a sense of peace pervaded. The meeting went on long past the appointed hour of dismissal, but when we finally walked out into the autumn sunshine, even those hurting most glowed with an awareness that God had met them. He wasn't going to let them go through their trials alone. The Lord would be the needed strength in the days ahead.

One particular verse became a personal promise to each of us, and as the days, months and years have passed, God remains faithful to His Word of hope.

> *"For I know the plans I have for you," declares the Lord, "plans to prosper and not to harm you, plans to give you hope and a future." (Jeremiah 29:11)*

I've found that as I focus on God's viewpoint and begin to see eye to eye with Him, my problems and those of my loved ones have less power to overwhelm me. When I don't see "how" to cope or help, I go to the Source of my strength to find the way. "You will keep in perfect peace him whose mind is steadfast, because he trusts in you. Trust in the Lord forever, for the Lord, the Lord, is the Rock eternal" (Isaiah 26:3-4).

Another of God's comforting words has also become reality for me. "Delight yourself in the Lord and he will give you the desires of your heart" (Psalm 37:4).

Desperation or delight?

Your positive example and influence does make a difference. It may not show up right away, or it may produce fruit immediately. With kids of any age, it is important to keep talking with them. Never give up. Accept them where they are. Love them.

It would be Pollyannaish to assume or pretend that entrusting God with long-lasting and hurtful problems, such as those women at our mountain retreat faced, takes away all the distress of the trial. There is still pain. There is still concern. Some see answers. Some don't. The problems may continue to exist; but in the midst of it all peace overcomes desperation. You no longer have to wonder what you are going to do when you leave both your children and your problems to the Lord. You can relax and simply trust. This doesn't mean we deny the problem. There are no false smiles. We simply accept the fact that "good" parents don't always have "perfect" children, and so we continue to love and pray for them.

Those who wait upon the Lord for His loving, sovereign will to be done soar on wings like eagles. They get a "higher" view and a new perspective. Those who, instead, focus on the problem and grovel in their disappointment are crushed and bitter.

I know. I've been both places.

My disagreement, disappointment and dismay over differences with grown-up children have taken me through a whole gamut of emotions. I've derided myself for not being a good enough mother. I've blamed God for not "making them turn out as I wished." I've allowed bitterness to keep me from reading the Bible and praying. I've been a smother-mother, an errant-parent, a cross-boss. In my most desperate moods, I've questioned my status, my sanity, and my salvation. But those experiences were not "dead ends" as I had first thought. They were God's detours leading to new discoveries in His kingdom.

During one of the times hurt feelings and disappointment had taken over my thinking, I came upon a word from God that He has often used to heal my life.

> *See to it that no one misses the grace of God and that no bitter root grows up to cause trouble and defile many. (Hebrews 12:15)*

What picturesque language. A bitter root. A "root of bitterness," it says in the King James Version. As I read those words, I could envision twisted and tangled roots—roots of bitterness—choking out the joy and love God wanted me to have. I had almost let those roots destroy me. And, as a sometime gardener, I knew how hard it was to pull roots out of dry ground. I didn't have the strength to do it. So . . . I called upon the only One who could help. "Lord," I prayed, "I've allowed the root of bitterness to strangle the life you've given. Please pull it out for me."

He did. And He does each and every time I ask.

God's pruning has sometimes been hard. When we can't see eye to eye with our children, and our eyes are turned inward (I call them ingrown eyeballs), the only hope for the future lies in lifting our eyes to God. Try it. You'll like it.

> *Humble yourselves, therefore, under God's mighty hand, that he may lift you up in due time. Cast all your anxiety on him because he cares for you. (I Peter 5:6-7)*

DISAGREE WITHOUT BEING DISAGREEABLE

Although there may be some problems in your family that equal or exceed those we've talked about, those disagreements that estrange can be of another variety. We may not approve of our child's mate, the way they raise their children, how they spend their money, or the church they do or don't attend. However, we need to face the fact that our approval or disapproval will probably make no difference in their choices. All it does is build a wall between us.

Lucille, one of my friends, was deeply hurt when Julie, her only child, changed churches. She embraced a belief that was different in many ways from that of her childhood. Julie proceeded to "preach at" her mother every opportune (and even inopportune) moment they were together, trying to convince her that over the past years she had been in error. The only hope, according to the daughter, was for her mother to change her beliefs. Lucille applied the only protection she had available: distance. The new religious affiliation and a new husband had taken Julie to another region to live, so Lucille made it a point not to visit and to call only when necessary. Her feelings and personal beliefs were too sensitive to allow her daughter to get close.

I did the same thing to my father when I became a Christian. In my evangelistic zeal, I not only drove him away from me, but also deeper into his own safety zone. Only in the last year have we been able to talk openly and freely without putting up offenses or defenses. He still has not accepted the Lord, but we've learned to disagree without being disagreeable. And I continue to pray for him.

Lucille and Julie learned this lesson after several years of estrangement. Today, still separated by miles and personal beliefs in God, they visit each other with enjoyment and respect. And, they do not discuss the things that divide them. They decided their relationship was more important than their differences.

It's important to be willing to give a little, to listen to others' opinions and to consider their feelings as well as defense mechanisms. We can be close to our adult children and our parents without having to agree on every issue. It's not our responsibility to change another's beliefs. Rather, we must stand honestly in our own convictions before God, embrace them with wholeheartedness, share our faith with loves ones, then leave the results with God. We owe them honesty and respect.

One way to disagree without becoming disagreeable is to focus upon the agreeable things.

In this way, we do not compromise our beliefs or convictions. We just accept them—and our family— where we are and for who we are. And then we go on together.

Maxine and her husband discovered this. Maxine was at the point of ripping out her hair (and her daughter's!) when she learned that her daughter had married and that her new son-in-law was of a different race. What would people think? What would their grandchildren look like? How would this young man be accepted into their conservative family?

But when Amy's parents met their new son-in-law, they worked at loving him. Eventually they began to see their son-in-law's fine character, and the family relationship blossomed. Amy, her husband, and her parents have built a relationship that has grown through three very beautiful grand-children and many years of happily married life.

By allowing their daughter the freedom to grow and develop her own opinion, their family has had the opportunity to deepen their adult relationships and grow together in their love and respect for each other . . . and for their adult differences of opinion.

As Mark Twain said, "Loyalty to a petrified opinion never yet broke a chain or freed a human soul."

FOR DISCUSSION AND ENCOURAGEMENT

- Is your disagreement with your child or a parent causing bitterness? Allow God to remove that root. Write down the problem. See it as a dry, shriveled root. Throw the piece of paper, along with the bitterness, into the trash where it belongs. Then ask God to replace those bitter thoughts with positive ones.

- Remember that prayer about serenity? Go back to chapter one and read it again. Can you change your child? Can you change yourself? As God for courage to change what you can and to accept what cannot be changed.

- On what can you and your adult child agree? You taste in music? clothes? friends? food? books? God? Instead of thinking about your disagreements, talk together about those things you have in common.

- Whether you have a super relationship with your grown-up kids or a dismal one, if time has passed without sharing feelings and concerns with your adult child, make the effort. Invite him/her to lunch. Go on a picnic or to a play. Make her something to wear. Make him something for his home. Several months ago, I made one of my sons a quilt for his bed. I was thrilled by his response! See what you can do to creatively say, "I love you."

- Memorize this verse.
  If anyone considers himself religious and yet does not keep a tight rein on his tongue, he deceives himself and his religion is worthless. (James 1:26)

- How can you apply it this week? With regard to your family situation, when should you?

But godliness with contentment is great gain. . . . Keep your lives free from the love of money and be content with what you have, because God has said, "Never will I leave you; never will I forsake you."—I Timothy 6:6; Hebrews 13:5

6

Money Bags

"Mommy, can I have a dime for candy?"

"Sure, honey."

"Mom, I need two dollars for lunch."

"Okay."

"I have to have forty dollars to rent a tux!"

"Here, take my charge card."

"Dad, all the guys have cars." "Mom, all the girls have cars."

"Do you think money grows on trees?"

"But I have to have the brakes fixed."

"Oh, all right, but there must be an end to this."

"You don't expect me to work and go to college, do you?"

"Mom and dad, we need a down payment for a house."

"The kids need braces."

"But you and dad have plenty of money. And we've never been to Hawaii!"

Is there an end to this? How much am I expected to help my children—my grown-up children?

A good question. How much financial aid should a parent give? Does the word "should" even belong in there? Perhaps it might be better to ask, "How much financial aid do I want to give my children?"

I was surprised, as I talked to many parents of adult children, to learn that this problem has been a major wedge in their relationships. The parents often feel used and unappreciated, and the children are confused by their attitudes. "Why didn't they say they didn't want to help out? Mom and dad both smiled when they wrote the check."

Sometimes it is hard to tell the difference between a grin and a grimace. If, as parents, we always had an open purse and have never learned to say, "No," we should not be surprised that our grown children still ask for money—and expect it. They may never have learned the pride in providing for their own needs. But it's never too late for them to learn, for their own good as well as yours.

Someone has said that the most valuable gift you can give another is a good example. If that is true, then we can genuinely help our children by teaching them independence. Then they, in turn, can inspire this quality in their children, and so on down through the generations. And that's an inheritance worth giving! It may be that either we or our parents were poor, and we've tried to keep our children from that kind of suffering. We may feel some kind of psychological or emotional need for control. We may have fallen into an over-protective type of mindset and we know we have to make a change. An Oriental proverb says, "If fate throws a knife at you, there are two ways to catch it: by the blade or by the handle."

Let's get a handle on our money bags.

I feel certain that those reading a book like this not only want to know how to cope with and enjoy their grown-up kids but they want what is best for them. You are caring parents who love your family; and you alone can make the decision to tighten your purse strings or to go on openhanding it. There are times when both approaches may be wise.

Parenthood doesn't end when our children move out on their own. We want—and need—to continue loving, enjoying and looking forward to those times we spend together. I once heard a man say, "You rarely succeed at anything unless you have fun doing it." I think that applies to this business of being a parent, too.

Do you enjoy your grown-up child?

Do you have fun together?

Or does every visit and phone call end in an argument and hurt feelings?

How much of that misery has its roots in money problems?

We need to face the truth: money does not buy love. "Oh, I know that," you say. But you'd be surprised how many people don't know it. A wealthy professional man I know buys his adult children VCRs, microwaves, large-screen TVs, and other expensive, adult "toys." In so doing, he manages to keep them dependent on him. They only come around when they want some new trinket, but, "they love me," he says, his chin in the air.

If they love their dad, it's in spite of, not because of, his lavish gifts. I hope he learns that soon because when he runs out of "things" to buy them, he will be a depressed man, unsure of his children's love.

Besides, have you noticed that the more you have, the more you want? To be in love with money or its offspring never satisfies. That's human nature, and God pinpointed this defect in us centuries ago.

> *For the love of money is a root of all kinds of evil. Some people, eager for money, have wandered from the faith and pierced themselves with many griefs. (I Timothy 6:10)*

> *Whoever loves money never has money enough; whoever loves wealth is never satisfied with his income. This too is meaningless. (Ecclesiastes 5:10)*

I wonder how many Christians have been affected by the mentality that says, "Love God and get rich" or "Send us your money, and God will bless you." It obviously works for them. Just look at the flashing diamonds and big homes these people have.

Does this attraction to a god who blesses men's desire for money and physical comfort play an important part in the way we and our children view riches?

Could it be that we are trying to play "god" in their lives?

How much financial aid should we give our children? That's a question only you can answer. An old Scottish proverb gives a little insight, though. "Ask thy purse what thou shouldst spend." If you have it and want to spend it on your children, that's your right. But if you love them, go easy. You *want* them to learn independence, too.

Some Case Histories

Since I don't claim to have all—or even half— the answers of what may be right for your family, I'll just share what we have done in ours. We've never been wealthy, and at times we've been below average in income. I suppose that at this point in our lives, we would be considered middle-class. We have an average home with average furniture. Some pieces need to be replaced, and when we're ready financially, we'll do it. Right now, we're still in the process of helping the last of our grown-up children complete her education.

We believe that if it is possible for us to give our children a college education and they want it, they should be able to attend school—a state university— full time without having to worry about room and board. Their dad says, "No use prolonging the agony. The sooner they get out of school, the sooner they can support themselves." And so this has been our policy.

However, each one of our children has also worked part time while attending school because they like the feeling of independence. And, to be honest, they like having some spending money.

When they begin college, we provide them with a car—not a new, fancy model, but something they like, with a low price tag and inexpensive maintenance. They are expected to pay for insurance, gas, oil, and minor upkeep. We take care of major repairs, tune-ups, and so on, until they graduate and are on their own. We have no unbendable rules, and when a son or daughter has needed extra help, we have done what we could. Several times when they were ready to repay the loan, we've said, "No, let us count it as a gift." Other times when we've believed their income was improving, we've accepted the money and thanked them. The pride on their faces at times like that was a blessing to us. These are financial decisions we've made for our family and for us, they've worked.

The "Trying Twenties" as Gail Sheehy calls these years in her book, *Passages,* is a time when our children are making the transition to full adulthood and transplanting their roots into a lifestyle of their own choosing. It is the privilege of parents to help them make this change smoothly and with confidence. Career, homes, marriage, children: these are only the outward adjustments to be made. Internally our grown-up kids struggle with self-image, choices, and relationships.

More and more young people are seeking counselors to help them develop confidence and a healthy self-esteem. I think if they see a need and can afford it, it's money well spent. From the positive results I've seen, I can't help but wish I had been able to work through some of my hang-ups with a Christian counselor instead of inflicting them on my family and friends. The insights and challenges of a counselor can offer valuable help and shortcuts to growth.

However, the learning process, though long, has been a good one for me. I found that my daily quiet time and prayer life were essential to my spiritual as well as emotional development. God's Word has an answer for every problem or fear I encounter. This personal quest just takes more time and a dedication to knowing and obeying what He shows us.

What does this have to do with money? Paying one's own way, resolving money problems, learning to live on what we have: these experiences build self-image, wisdom of choice, and yes, even relationships.

Adult children who make their own car payments, buy their own furniture, and supply the needs of their own families have truly matured when they can balance those needs within the framework of good financial stewardship. They are no longer shortsighted "kids," but "grown-ups" who plan and budget—and may even have money left at the end of the month.

How Much is Enough?

What if we're trying to provide for ourselves or for our grown-up kids? Ease? Happiness? Contentment? The Apostle Paul wrote:

> *I know what it is to be in need, and I know what it is to have plenty. I have learned the secret of being content in any and every situation, whether well fed or hungry, whether living in plenty or in want. I can do everything through him who gives me strength. (Philippians 4:12-13)*

A vital relationship with Christ is the answer to contentment. Money can't buy that. And, as Paul told Timothy, "But godliness with contentment is great gain. For we brought nothing into the world, and we can take nothing out of it" (I Timothy 6:6-7).

A true perspective on eternal values will change our attitude toward the striving and ambitions that may rule our lives. Neither we nor our children arrived on this earth with fine clothes and fancy jewelry . . . and we all know we can't take it with us. If this is a problem area, begin today to practice a new and realistic attitude toward your finances. It may change your life, and there may still be time to pass this on to your children. Example does speak louder than words.

LOOSEN THE STRINGS . . .

On your apron, not your purse. Encourage your children to grow in independence as they make decisions and face the responsibilities of managing their own money wisely. As they mature in your home as pre-teens and teens, warn them of the danger of overextending credit, living beyond their income, or getting caught up in materialism and greed. With adult children you can offer the same warnings. Be honest with them about the responsibility that money imposes. Show them by example that contentment isn't a by-product of wealth or things but a sense of dependence upon God's will and purpose for their lives. Encourage them to "seek first his kingdom and his righteousness. . . ." (Matthew 6:33)

And remember, the lessons that will stay with them the longest and further them most in their growth to maturity are the ones they learn through experience. It's hard to see them weather those cold winds, but you taught them when they were small how to button their coats. Give them the chance to do it now.

DISCUSSION AND ENCOURAGEMENT

- What new thoughts have you gleaned from reading this chapter? Try to put them in writing.

- What positive solution are you going to apply with your children when they ask for money?

- Why do you think your grown-up kids are unrealistic about money management? Be honest. Have you handled your money wisely?

- Are you an impulse buyer? Are your children? Would you be willing to take steps to change that habit in your own life?

- What rights have you given to Jesus Christ

as the Lord of your income? Encourage your children to seek Christ's wisdom in money matters as they begin life outside the family home.

- List five things, excluding money, that give you contentment. Thank God for them.

Man must cease attributing his problems to his environment, and learn again to exercise his will—his personal responsibility in the realm of faith and morals.—Albert Schweitzer

7

Careful Confrontation

Because we don't have a clearly defined understanding of the difference between correction and confrontation, this may be one of the most difficult issues parents and adult children face. But our wisdom in knowing when to confront—and how—can strengthen our love and friendship with both our children and our parents.

I'm just learning to face a difficulty instead of running away or barging through it. And the process isn't easy for me as an adult child or as the parent of adult children. My mistake has been to either comfort or correct when I saw a problem. After all, that's the way I handled thorny situations when my children were growing up. It's hard to change!

"Hey, fella, didn't you forget to say, 'Thank you?'"

"I'm sorry, Mom. Thanks for finding my baseball mitt."

"Honey, don't feel so bad about losing this contest. There will be others."

Correcting. Comforting.

But now those children are grown-up and free from my parental training. It's no longer my position to tell them to say "Thank you," and "You're welcome." If they still have bad manners, I won't punish them. I can't force them to come back into the room and sit on a chair until they're ready to be polite. Correction (to set right by altering or adjusting; to point out faults; to punish) is no longer my responsibility. But I do have the right—and the obligation—to lovingly confront (come face to face with) a problem.

So how about comforting? Isn't that still a parental trust. Yes, when comfort is needed. But often our adult children don't need comfort in their personal relationships. They need confrontation.

"Bill is so insensitive to my needs. All he wants to do is stay home and putter around the yard on Saturdays, and I'd like to go to a play in the city."

"Connie is so dull. All she can talk about is what the kids have been doing all day. Where is that exciting woman I married?"

"Bill is insensitive. You deserve so much more."

"And Connie—just because she has three pre-schoolers is no excuse to let her mind go."

Comfort?

Those kinds of responses only breed more discontent, and can send our children off to a divorce lawyer. What these adults need is some good, old-fashioned, mature confrontation. We cannot correct or comfort their thinking, but we can face them with it. For instance, a loving, confrontive approach might be, "Are you sensitive to Bill's needs? Maybe if you'd putter around the garden with him on Saturday mornings, he would putter around with you on Saturday nights."

"Well, son, I can't attempt to change your attitude, but face it, those are your children, too. Have you considered keeping the kids and giving Connie a night out to take some classes or attend a concert? Talking to waist-high people all day isn't exactly stimulating."

You get the idea. We don't try to change our grown-up kids, but we can show them the possibility of changing themselves. We confront. The rest is up to them. If the advice is unsolicited, pray much and speak gently before treading on what might be sensitive ground.

WHEN TO CONFRONT

Knowing when to face a loved one with a problem can be as confusing as knowing how. For instance, Fran has grown-up kids, and she and Harry are careful not to intrude in their lives. They respect the privacy of their married children and allow them freedom and distance, but. . . .

"Sometimes our children think we're not interested in them when we don't ask questions or drop in uninvited," she says. "We don't offer advice, and they have translated that as 'not caring.'"

That's a common problem among parents who bend too far in not interfering. My own daughter confronted me along this line a few days ago.

"Mom, I don't want to hurt your feelings, but something's been bothering me for awhile, and I want to talk about it."

Hmm. I felt a prickle up my back, then sent an arrow prayer: *Lord, help me to really hear what she's saying and respond in your Spirit.*

"Sometimes I feel like you just don't care about me anymore. You don't come over to see me, and you never call. I just feel left out. That's all."

I listened and watched in amazement as tears oozed up in her large blue eyes and spilled over onto her cheeks. She wanted me to come over? She wanted me to call? But I thought she and her new husband preferred their privacy on evenings and weekends. I had no idea. . . .

After we discussed why I hadn't "intruded" on her time, she realized that I was only trying to be considerate, and I discovered that although she did value her privacy, my occasional visit or call was more than welcome.

She confronted. I gained new insight.

She had chosen the right moment to speak to me about her feelings. If she had waited longer, her misunderstanding of my motives would have grown, and I wouldn't have known that she missed my companionship! I'm so glad she confronted me.

Even though I am a parent, I am also my mother's grown-up kid. She confronted me this past week.

We've always been extremely close. She and my

dad divorced when I was thirteen, and my growing up years were spent with a "single" mother. We shared secrets, clothes and interests. Years later, when we had both married and come to a personal relationship with Christ, our attachment grew. We have enjoyed Christian fellowship and a friendship that is unique between mother and daughter. However, our like-mindedness has taken a turn lately, and though we've felt it, we hesitated to talk about it.

We both still love Christ and live totally for Him. We are actively involved in our churches and serve the Lord wholeheartedly. In the past two years, though, Mother has been attending a church whose doctrine differs somewhat from what we originally believed. She is excited and enthusiastic about the new things she is seeing and hearing. Because she loves me, her desire is that I accept what has brought her joy.

I've listened, somewhat skeptically, and have felt unhappy that we no longer believe exactly the same way. I've tried to hide my feelings from her, but she knows me well. Too well.

"There's something between us, and it makes me sad," she said one day over lunch.

I continued to toy with my salad and let my gaze wander over the other patrons in the restaurant.

"I want us to be like we've always been," she added, "able to share everything."

This was the time. We had to confront and accept the difference between us. We are individuals. She has a right to change, and so do I. As growing adults, we realized that even though we may not believe exactly the same, we can still respect each other's right to follow the convictions of her own heart. We discussed our differences and our similarities. We hugged and felt a new sense of freedom in our relationship.

I'm glad she was bold enough to confront without correction. I'm glad I was bold enough to confront without comfort. The time was right. The words were right. The outcome? We have given each other and ourselves permission to continue growing . . . in God's way and will.

When Peter saw him [John], he asked, "Lord, what about him?"

> *Jesus answered, "If I want him to remain alive until I return, what is that to you? You must follow me." (John 21:21-22)*

"You must follow me." Let's not be cross-eyed believers with one eye on Jesus and the other on those around us. Follow Him!

When to confront? David Augsburger in his book, *Caring Enough To Confront,* writes, "When confronting, focus feedback not on the easiest time and place to suit your own schedule but on the best time and the optimal situation for the receiver."

In other words, be thoughtful, kind, and loving. Take into consideration the other person's mood, time frame and concentration level.

I can't count the times I've chosen the wrong moment to confront my husband. If he's reading the paper, watching a football game, or involved in photographing a bird in flight, I wait. Our grown-up kids deserve the same consideration, and so do our parents. Know when and when not to confront.

HOW TO CONFRONT

With righteous indignation? With cool authority? With a look of, "How could you hurt your mother like this?"

David Augsburger points out that, "When situations of conflict become difficult, I want to speak clearly, honestly, personally, directly, in simple statements."

That's easier said than done for many of us. If we've been taught to always give in or to veil unpleasant truths with selective honesty, we will find confrontation both hard to give and hard to accept. We will skirt around issues and avoid facing problems. "Peace at any price" becomes our motto. But isn't that the same banner flying over depressed and disillusioned nations? Isn't that equivalent to a doormat mentality?

If you find it more painful than pulling teeth to be confrontive, read *Caring Enough to Confront*. It will help you build stronger relationships with your mate, your parents, your grown-up children, and even with your friends and church leaders.

AFTER THE "WHEN" AND "HOW"

The moment felt right. Our son and his wife were about to begin the second leg of their voyage. The first hadn't gone so well. She had suffered with seasickness and he was depressed, thinking that the work and planning of years might have to be aborted. I had a moment alone with him, the joy and pride of my life, and as I gave him a goodbye hug, I whispered so only he could hear, "Son, please remember that although your wife can work alongside you like a man, she is a woman. Treat her with consideration and gentleness. Love and encourage her."

He smiled with understanding, gave me a squeeze, and his father and I waved as they sailed out of sight.

The time was right. The motive was right. The words were simple and straightforward. Now what?

"A man convinced against his will is not convinced." How true.

If that son accepts the confrontation, and if he acts on what was said, good. Good for his wife. Good for him. But if he chooses to be selfish and inconsiderate, that is also his choice. We do not change people. God changes them. And people change themselves as they feel the need for change.

It may be—in fact, it's likely—that someone other than you will be instrumental in showing your adult children the error of their ways. A six-year-old girl confronted one of my sons.

"Do you ever eat?" she asked.

"What do you mean do I ever eat?"

"All I ever see you do is drink beer."

Confrontation.

A few weeks later, a peer echoed the same sentiments. "Do you think you may have a drinking problem?"

"Why do you say that?"

"I'm still sipping on my first beer and you just started your sixth!"

Confrontation. First, a little girl, then an older one. He heard, but he didn't listen.

He rode his motorcycle down a narrow road late at night. Suddenly the moon disappeared. The darkness became thick and heavy. He awoke at the side of the road under the bike. There was no voice this time, but the confrontation was there. This time he listened. He admitted himself into a treatment program. Today he is growing. He is once again sensitive to God, to others, to himself. But there has been much pain for him and for those who love him.

I sometimes wonder what would have happened if I had known he had a drinking problem. Would I have confronted? Would he have listened?

Learn when and how to confront your grownup kids, and learn how to receive confrontation, too. Then leave the results with God. Accept responsibility for yourself, and let your children do the same. We have to quit blaming ourselves and others for our circumstances, and make our choices based on God's Word and will. We can do only so much for our children. Then we must leave the results, decisions and actions to them.

If your brother sins, rebuke him, and if he repents, forgive him. If he sins against you seven times in a day, and seven times comes back to you and says, "I repent," forgive him. (Luke 17:3)

Brothers, if someone is caught in a sin, you who are spiritual should restore him gently. But watch yourself, or you also may be tempted. Carry each other's burdens, and in this way you will fulfill the law of Christ. (Galatians 6:1-2)

FOR DISCUSSION AND ENCOURAGEMENT

- Do you see your adult children making serious mistakes? Try to see those same "mistakes" through their eyes. How does that change the perspective?

- If there really is a problem, approach your child as a friend—with consideration for his feelings and time.

- State your thoughts simply, honestly and with compassion. Be sure your child understands what it is you are saying, that you are not attacking her, but only pointing out a problem.

- Don't argue or defend your position. You are not trying to change or challenge them. You are only making an observation.

- Don't get your feelings hurt if your words are rejected. You have not been rejected. Leave the results with God.

- These same points may be applied to your parents. Don't be rude or condescending. You are an adult, and so are they. Behave in a mature manner.

Through Jesus, therefore, let us continually offer to God a sacrifice of praise—the fruit of lips that confess his name. And do not forget to do good and to share with others, for with such sacrifices God is pleased.—Hebrews 13:15-16

8

Balm Not Blame

"SEE WHAT YOU MADE me do!"

How many times have you heard that one? Or maybe even said it yourself? I was constantly amazed at how quickly the children would offer information when I asked, "Who broke this glass?" Or, "Why is your sister crying?"

"He made me do it."

"Becky climbed up on the chair and. . . ."

"Danny pushed me."

"Kathy wouldn't let me have it."

And on and on. It was always someone else who did it, said it, or caused it.

Sometimes parents have to be super sleuths in order to discern, "Who done it." Sometimes we misjudged, and the wrong person was blamed and sent to her room. Once in awhile a little sister with red eyes and nose confessed, but more often than not, there was blame. That habit of accusing—and excusing ourselves—goes on into adulthood. We're sure that our problems are really the result of another's ineptness or foolishness.

"I wouldn't have a weight problem if my children didn't love sweets so much," says a plump mother tasting cookie dough.

"I could be more patient if everyone else would stay out of my way," says a dad leaning on the horn of his car.

I'm sure you're familiar with the excuses we all make now and then. Even made a few yourself, huh?

But have you blamed your grown-up kids for your unhappiness? Have you blamed yourself for their unhappiness? I've done both. Instead of applying a soothing balm to heal an emotional hurt, I either caused more pain by blaming them, or applied a spiritual Band-Aid by blaming myself and withdrawing into a quiet corner to sulk. Not pretty.

When our oldest son strayed away from the precepts of the family and embraced the hippie culture, I was miserable. I cried. I moped. I complained. I blamed him . . . and God.

"Oh, Lord," I prayed, "why did this happen to me?" (Translation: I think you slipped up somewhere along the line. I did my part, but you didn't do yours.) Hadn't I been a stay-at-home-mother? I even baked oatmeal cookies and fixed hot chocolate to welcome the children home from school. I took them to Sunday School, read them Bible stories and prayed with them before bedtime. I did all that—and still. . . .

I was so full of self and self-righteous ways that I couldn't see God's loving hand in this difficult situation.

"Why?" "Why me?" I moaned

Although I didn't realize it at the time, I was blaming God. Charles Swindoll in Strengthening Your Grip says, "If we choose to blame God, we cut off our single source of power." How true that is! During those days I went round and round in circles before I finally stopped blaming and began to accept the balm of God's Word.

I also blamed my son for my misery. "Why is he behaving this way? Doesn't he appreciate all we've done for him?" I was hurt and angry that he had chosen a lifestyle so opposed to his early training.

But that wasn't all. I blamed myself. "If only I had . . ." "Maybe I should have . . ." I was listening to the flip side of the same record entitled "Self-Pity." This attitude brought gloom on my other children as I poured my worry and anguish out on anyone who would listen. Then one day a change took place.

God applied His Word to my pain. At first His medicine stung, like the bright red Merthiolate my mother had dabbed on my eight-year-old skinned knees. But after awhile, the pain subsided and healing began. My tears were exchanged for a quiet hope and my words of complaint to praise.

"Give thanks in all circumstances, for this is God's

will for you in Christ Jesus." (I Thessalonians 5:18)

Ouch! Give thanks in this situation? How could I thank God when I felt so unthankful? It would be hypocrisy for me to say, "Thank you, Lord." Or would it? If I began thanking Him, I would no longer blame. If I thanked God in my circumstances, I couldn't enjoy my self-pity anymore.

"This is God's will for you in Christ Jesus."

So one day I surrendered and said, "Thank you, Lord. Thank you for my son who is so precious to me. You love him even more than I do. Thank you for your eternal plan. I can't see the end from the beginning, but it's all the same to you. Thank you."

I hoped God wouldn't notice that I didn't feel thankful. I was only saying the words. They didn't come from my heart—only my mouth.

But something wonderful was taking place not only inside me, but also in my husband as he, too, prayed for our son. As we thanked God for His wisdom and love, our emotions began lining up with our words. The act of obedience to God's Word, by faith, had turned our confusion into joyful response. As the prophet Samuel said:

> *Does the Lord delight in burnt offerings and sacrifices as much as in obeying the voice of the Lord? To obey is better than sacrifice, and to heed is better than the fat of rams. (I Samuel 15:22)*

God *does* know what is best! God is in this circumstance! God *does* have a plan for my child— for me—and for our entire family.

It took three years, but during that time, our firstborn child was drawn back into fellowship with us and the Lord. And we all grew during those confusing days. We learned that although God's ways are not our ways, they are best.

Will you thank Him in your present situation? Will you trust Him with your life and the lives of your children? Will you exercise the same patience toward God that He does toward you?

And did you catch that word "will?" It seems to boil down to that. Even when we don't feel like loving or thanking, we can will ourselves to do so. We can choose consciously what our response will be. Our will, controlled by the Holy Spirit, is the driving force of our lives, yet we often think our emotions are, and we allow them to dictate our responses. Put the will to work, though, and watch the emotions come under control.

The Word of God combined with faith truly is a balm—a soothing ointment—for our hurt spirits. However, we have a choice. Will we apply the balm or continue to blame?

THE BLAME GAME

It's too bad we have to keep learning the same lessons over and over. I thought after my son returned to the Lord, I would never again forget to "give thanks in every circumstance." But I did. I had learned to play the "blame game" so well that it had become second nature.

If I was in a bad mood, it was my husband's fault. Just because he had a hard day at the office and was a little cross, I took it as my right to be cross, too.

It was my parents' fault I was overweight. If they hadn't made me clean up my plate as a child, I wouldn't still feel compelled to eat every last bit.

It was the pastor's fault that I felt depressed. Why did he have to preach on a subject I was sensitive about?

It was the government's fault that I didn't have all the material things I wanted. Such high taxes!

On and on the list goes: the kids, the neighbors, the clerks, the people on welfare. You name it—most of us can find someone else to blame for our situation, attitude or circumstances. Charles Swindoll wrote, ". . . not until we stop blaming will we start enjoying health and happiness again!" *(Strengthening Your Grip)*

As long as we blame anyone or anything else for our problems, we cannot be helped. We must accept responsibility, without self-pity, for those things we have caused; attempt to make amends; thank God for His perfect will and wisdom—and move on.

I was afraid that the son who is recovering from alcoholism blamed us somehow for his problem. I thought, "Maybe we were too strict about our rules against drinking." Or, "Was I so hard on him during his adolescence that he turned to drink?"

I went to him, confessing some of the times I had overreacted and punished him unjustly. I cried on his shoulder. "Oh, I'm sorry I wasn't a better mother."

My son focused his dark brown eyes on me and spoke softly. "Mom, don't blame yourself for this. I brought it on myself, and now I'm doing something about it."

Such maturity. I'm amazed at what I'm learning from him. He doesn't blame. He doesn't indulge in self-pity. Through the "Twelve Steps" of Alcoholics Anonymous, he is learning to live one day at a time without blame—without shame.

BALM OR BOMB?

There are at least two ways we can use the Word of God with our grown-up kids. If we see them doing something we're sure is wrong, we can "bomb" them with the Word, or "balm" them with it. Whichever method we choose will determine the kind of relationship we have with each other.

Choose? Yes. There's that word again. That means I have to think before I speak, even perhaps pray, "Lord, I see my adult child choosing the wrong path. Should I rebuke him with, 'Be sure your sin will find you out?' or would the words, '. . . in all your ways acknowledge him, and he shall direct your paths,' be the best choice?"

As parents of adult children we frequently stand at the crossroads. I love my child. I want not only what's best for him, but I want what's best for me, too. A rebuke given in the spirit of love may be what is needed. I can think of many times my mother has rebuked her grown-up kid with a strong word. It hurt, but I knew it was in love and what I needed. She did not bomb me with it, but administered the Word as a doctor would a strong medicine.

If we want a close friendship with our grown-up

kids, we must choose carefully the words we speak. Not blame . . . not bomb . . . but balm.

> *My dear brothers, take note of this: Everyone should be quick to listen, slow to speak and slow to become angry, for man's anger does not bring about the righteous life that God desires. (James 1:19-20)*

FOR DISCUSSION AND ENCOURAGEMENT

- Have you blamed someone today for a problem? Think about it awhile. It may have been spoken or only a thought.

- Was that person really to blame? What could you have done to avoid the problem?

- Is your grown-up child facing a serious trial? Are you at fault? Is he/she? Is there anything you can do? Ask God to give you His attitude in this situation.

- Do you believe Charles Swindoll's words about cutting off our source of power when we blame God? Can you think of an example in yours or someone else's life to support that statement?

- Will you, by faith, thank God in your present circumstance? Voice that obedience aloud. Continue to thank Him. Acknowledge His will and sovereignty. God never makes mistakes.

And now these three remain: faith, hope and love. But the greatest of these is love.
                    —I Corinthians 13:13

9

The Love Connection

WE TALK ABOUT LOVE. We read about love. We even claim to love. But what is this thing called love? Is it the warm fuzzies? or a shivery tingle up the spine? If so, how can we tell the difference between love and a case of the flu?

Believe it or not, the preceding chapters have all been about love. We've talked about acceptance, maturity, support, disagreeing without being disagreeable, financial help, confrontation, and applying the balm of God's Word. This is love in action. We do love our grown-up kids. What we want to learn is how to express that love in a manner that will be a maturing experience for both children and parents.

In the past, we may have believed the way to show love is to give . . . give . . . give. And that certainly is an important aspect of love. But when and how should we give? and what? These are questions we all have.

M. Scott Peck in *The Road Less Traveled* wrote, "Love is not simply giving; it is judicious giving and judicious withholding as well." He goes on to say, as we have already considered, that love includes confrontation, struggle, urging, praising, and even criticism. Love involves leadership and decision making. And, as parents of young children or grown-up kids, we have to make some hard choices. Does my child need comfort or confrontation? Is there a need for praise or a push? Am I equipped to meet those needs? Perhaps the choice is not mine this time.

I've had to face my reactions to my family as they've grown up. Often I sacrificed my own well-being and choices in order to meet their needs. While they were children, this was necessary; but to continue in a self-sacrificing way of life is not healthy for me or my children. To give in to their every whim and expectation keeps them infants, dependent on me, and it can make me a martyr-mom. Sometimes I may appear to be unfeeling when I say, "No. I can't spare the time today." I believe, though, that the love and respect between me and my children is more genuine now than it would have been if I had continued to be their "provider."

What we need to ask ourselves as parents of adult kids is, "Am I taking on this activity which demands self-sacrifice because I love my children or because I want to project an image of a 'good' person or 'the perfect parent'?" Remember Alice and Toni? Alice thought she was showing her love for her daughter when she allowed herself to be used. But when we genuinely love, it's because we want to, not because we feel we must. Love is so much more than a feeling. It's a being. Love begins in the will and is one of those decisions we make. To love or not to love: that is the connection.

THE LOVE CONNECTION

Now is a good time to restate that the purpose of this book is to help us as parents establish warm and loving relationships with our grown-up kids. There are thousands of mothers and fathers who enjoy their adult children, but there are thousands more heartbroken and disillusioned families who long for those close ties. Many men and women avoid their elderly parents because they feel they were let down or hurt years ago beyond forgiveness.

There's a dad whose only son didn't go into the family business as he had hoped. To his father's grief, the son chose an entirely different position. Those two men haven't shared a holiday or friendly conversation in five years. Ebenezer Scrooge had nothing on that father. Instead of a love connection, those families are allowing grudges to build solid, unclimbable walls.

It could be that you've become a grudge holder too. Some carry the excess baggage of, "I've done so much for my kids; and what did it get me?"

There are several things grudges can get you: illness, loss of self-esteem, intolerance, suspiciousness and hypersensitivity are a few. Psychologist Herbert J. Freudenberger says, "Consistent grudges can lead to stress, and everything from backaches to chest pains." He added that they can also damage friend-ships, family relationships and work positions. Other psychologists note that a grudge can be used as a punishment against someone or as a protection against intimacy. Fear of expressing anger or acknowledging vulnerability may be the root of a grudge-carrier's burden.

What can be done to mend the broken lines of that connection? Judy Eidelson, clinical director of the Institute of Cognitive Behavioral Therapy in Philadelphia, suggests that a grudge holder try to see the situation from the other person's perspective. Did your grown-up child respond the way he did because of his fear or insecurity? Why not ask him? Weigh the seriousness of the offense. Is the grudge you carry a reflection of your own personal immaturity or insecurity rather than a true perception of the problem? If you find it too difficult to talk about the grudge, try expressing it in a letter. It may be that just the act of writing your feelings down will be enough. You can throw the letter away and, having analyzed the situation, reach out in love to your child. Then work on acceptance of the situation. There are some things, some past hurts and experiences, that cannot be changed, but we need to forgive and move on to positive living.

> *. . . But one thing I do: Forgetting what is behind and straining toward what is ahead, I press on toward the goal to win the prize for which God has called me*

heavenward in Christ Jesus. (Philippians 3:13-14)

THE FORGIVENESS HABIT

A close friend dropped by the house one night. While we chatted over a cup of coffee, I noticed that her eyes were circled with red, and every now and then, she inhaled deeply. She was on the verge of tears when she finally came to the point of her visit. "Oh, I really need prayer." Her head swung to the right and she blinked a few times before continuing.

"I can't believe this is happening . . . again!"

I waited until she pulled a tissue from her purse and wiped the corners of her eyes.

"I thought this marriage would be different, but it's happening all over again."

I hadn't known Julie very long, but she had once shared that her first marriage had been a disaster. It had taken six years of solitary struggle, trying to advance in her job and to be a good mother to her little girl, before she found "Mr. Perfect."

Her second marriage would last. There was no doubt in Julie's mind. Darren was a Christian—a new one—and was excited about becoming a husband and father with the simple words, "I do." The first three years of married life had gone well as far as outsiders could see. But Julie had been holding onto some hurts from her previous marriage that were now threatening her happiness and even her future with Darren.

"Why?" she repeated. "Why is this happening to

me . . . again?"

As she shared the concern she felt for her marriage, I was glad she kept the particulars of their problems between her and her husband. She did share with me that she had learned something about him that hurt her deeply. Although they had talked it over and he had even asked her forgiveness, she felt betrayed and crushed. Her conversation kept returning to the past and the way her first husband had hurt her. "I can't stand to be hurt again," she repeated several times. "Darren promised that we would have family devotions together, and now he refuses to even pray with me. He makes excuses every Sunday not to go to church. Oh, he'll take Amy to Sunday school and go back to pick her up, but. . . ."

Married life with Darren was not what Julie had expected. She longed for a Christian home, for a warm companionship, and for her own dreams to be fulfilled, but Darren had let her down. She went on to tell how he had, from the beginning, reneged on his vows to take the spiritual lead in the family. She was disillusioned, disappointed, and unforgiving.

When she related that Darren had asked her forgiveness for this latest problem, she admitted that she hadn't forgiven him. A new understanding lit her eyes as she talked. "You know, I think I've held every single misunderstanding we've had since the day we were married against him. I've never forgiven him for anything!" She seemed amazed by her own confession. "I've allowed each argument and disagreement to grow in my heart until I feel I'm about to explode."

I drew in a deep breath, then told her of a lesson the Lord had taught me in forgiveness. One day when I was out jogging around the neighborhood, an incident which had happened many years before came to mind. It wasn't the first time I had mulled it over, though it had taken place almost thirty years ago. My husband had said something to me that hurt deeply. I felt he had been deliberately unkind in his remark, and ever so often I pulled those words out of my subconscious and chewed them over.

With each pounding step, I rehashed that scene and congratulated myself on my own superiority. "I would never say such a thing to someone I loved!" I told myself. Then, also out of the recesses of my memory, a Bible story emerged. When teaching on forgiveness, Jesus had admonished Peter that seven times was not enough to forgive someone who had sinned against him. *"I tell you, not seven times, but seventy-seven times."* (Matthew 18:21-22)

That day, I had a new understand of Jesus' words. He was not only alluding to a person who had sinned against us seventy-seven times, but to the fact that the same old grievance may arise in our minds seventy-seven times; and we are to *forgive it* again and again! Maybe after a while, we'll be willing to forget it, too.

That day Julie realized that not only had she been holding grudges against Darren, but she had also heaped the sins of her first husband onto his head. Before she left, we prayed together, and the expression on her face was a total change. The situation hadn't changed at home. Her husband was the same man she had left that morning. But Julie was no longer the same. She had experienced once again God's cleansing of her judgmental and unforgiving attitude, and she was filled with a realistic hope for the future. She called me the next day.

"Darren loves me, I know. And I love him. I'll just have to remember to forgive as I've been forgiven and let the Lord have complete control over our marriage. Our relationship isn't what I'd hoped it would be, but at least I'm not holding a grudge anymore."

Vincent P. Collins wrote in his pamphlet, "Acceptance," that we make a mistake in thinking that happiness comes from having our wants and desires satisfied. He said, "Actually, it consists in the serenity that comes from conforming our own will to the Will of God."

These same principles apply between parents and children—no matter how old they are. We know that God's will is that we love and forgive. To do that fully we must lay aside those resentments that separate us from our parents, our grown-up kids—or anyone else—and begin to do God's will. Just as we can will *to love*, we also will *to forgive*. Only in the exercise of this willfulness can we experience the love connection that binds parents to their adult children, both as friends and as equals. Actual case histories have shown that parents who refuse to risk rejection by stepping out in love and forgiveness choose a path of loneliness and senility. Their children go on with their lives. The grudge carriers are the losers.

Therefore, as God's chosen people, holy and dearly loved, clothe yourselves with compassion, kindness, humility, gentleness and patience. Bear with each other and forgive whatever grievances you may have against one another. Forgive as the Lord forgave you. And over all these virtues put on love, which binds them all together in perfect unity. (Colossians 3:12-14)

Whenever I think of familial forgiveness, Joseph comes to mind. This Old Testament hero is one of my favorites in the entire Bible. I can't read the portion about his supplying food to his brothers without crying. You remember the story: Joseph, because of his brothers' jealousy, was sold into Egypt. There, although he faced many trials and eventually prison, he continued to trust in God. Finally, years later as an honored and high-ranking official, Joseph had the responsibility (and privilege!) to distribute food to his destitute brothers who had come all the way from Israel. When he saw them after those many years, his heart broke with love for them.

No grudges.

No animosity.

When at last he revealed to them who he was, they were terrified. After what they had done to him, they knew they deserved his wrath . . . even revenge . . . perhaps death. But Joseph said:

> . . . *Do not be distressed and do not be angry with yourselves for selling me here,*

*because it was to save lives that God sent me
ahead of you. . . . It was not you who sent
me here, but God. (Genesis 45:5-8)*

God sent me ahead of you (v. 5). Joseph didn't blame them for what they had done; instead, he acknowledged the sovereign Lord who controls every detail of our lives.

Do you recognize God's gracious work in your life? Will you acknowledge His wisdom, love, provision, and sovereignty?

In your life?

In the lives of your grown-up kids?

FOR DISCUSSION AND ENCOURAGEMENT

- Is there any kind of separation between you and your adult children? Is it only a little "tiff," or are you holding a grudge? Be honest.

- Visualize your life a year or two from now. Look further into the future and envision yourself as an old man or woman . . . lonely and without friends. Is that kind of future worth your holding resentments?

- Has your child really hurt you? Or have you tried to take responsibility for his life, and your "gentle interference" has been unappreciated?

- Write a letter to your child. You aren't going to mail it, so be totally truthful about your feelings and desire to connect. Read it aloud before the Lord. Ask God to make your words a reality.

- This is the hardest part. Allow God to forgive you for your attitude and then, by an act of your will, forgive your child. Now ask God to help you forgive yourself.

- Call your child. Tell him you respect his rights as an adult; that you would like to try to reestablish a relationship. Ask his forgiveness for specific problems you may have had. Then leave the results with God. Your child may be as afraid as you are and hold back for awhile to test your sincerity. Give him time. Love him. Love him with Christ's love. That's the only love that lasts.

- Is the rift between you and a parent? Apply the same steps above and, as you talk to your earthly parent, thank your heavenly parent for His eternal love, understanding, and forgiveness.

In order that all men may be taught to speak truth, it is necessary that all likewise should learn to hear it.—Samuel Johnson

10

Talk Isn't Cheap

Have you ever told a special person something you were excited about, or worried about, or perplexed about and felt that they didn't hear? Silly question. We've all been on both sides of that situation. A husband, wife or child communicates with words, but they fall on deaf ears. The listener may appear to hear; the eyes are open and pointed in our direction, but even as we speak, we know they've tuned us out. If our sensitive natures are treated this way often enough, we may eventually quit sharing ourselves and withdraw, or we may express anger and frustration in ways that are not healthy. When the lines of communication are broken, so is the relationship.

This may be the problem between us and our grown-up kids. About the time they entered high school, we may have stopped listening, and so did they. The changes taking place in our teenagers were too hard to accept. No longer did cute little chubby-faced boys and girls run to us with open arms. Now long, sullen faces lift eyebrows in disgust and peer at us over thick, gooey slices of pizza. And it's no wonder those teens don't hear anything we say. The music piped into their ears through tiny earphones drowns out every other sound.

So. . . .

We stop talking.

And listening.

Parents usually express surprise when their children reach this stage. "I can't understand it. Jon and Lisa have changed. They just aren't the same children they used to be. It must be their school (friends, music, teachers). We once had such fun together, and now they don't even want to be with us."

Why?

Because they did change. And so does everything and everyone courageous enough to grow. Perhaps the real issue between parents and teens is that those kids are growing, and we aren't willing to adjust to meet their changing needs. We all know parents, and we may be in that group, who related well with their children until they were grown. I've known some moms and dads who even sailed through their kids' high school days on smooth seas, only to flounder and sink when their children left home, married, and began to live their own ideas.

How can we reconnect lines that are frayed and

even broken? Is it possible to face our conflicts and resolve them? Yes!

But we have to talk. We have to listen. And it's going to cost.

TALK ISN'T CHEAP

At least the kind of talk that gets down to issues isn't cheap. Sometimes it costs our pride. It costs time and tears. It may even cost, for a period, a deeper rift in the relationship. And this kind of talk takes two, a speaker and a listener, who are willing to switch positions throughout the course of the conversation.

If you are the instigator in trying to mend the torn lines of communication with your grown-up child or an older parent, make it clear at the outset that you have some things to say that are important to you. Then, also make it clear that you are willing to listen with an open mind to what he or she has to say. Before beginning, be sure both of you agree to talk *and* listen, and you both agree that a friendship between the two of you is important to both.

So often when we communicate, we think we're getting our message across by the tone of our voice or the way we wrinkle our brow. But much of the misunderstanding between people who love each other occurs because we "just think they know." We don't really say what we mean, and then we misinterpret the messages we hear. We need to weigh the words we speak and the words we hear carefully before responding or becoming emotional.

Let's look first at the way we talk. Suppose your

daughter has disappointed you time and again. Whenever you are together, you make small talk, trying to avoid an argument or the pain a confrontation may bring. You think she's ruining her life by the way she's living, and you know she's ruining yours! The hedging has gone on for months; you want to get this painful issue out in the open, and to your surprise, you discover she wants the same thing.

Before you begin your conversation, be sure you know what it is you want to say. Don't just barge into a soliloquy on your likes and dislikes. Avoid vagueness by choosing your words carefully and prayerfully. Words can pierce like arrows or soothe like ointment. Remember Proverbs 25:11? "A word aptly spoken is like apples of gold in settings of silver." And Proverbs 15:1 counsels, "A gentle answer turns away wrath, but a harsh word stirs up anger."

Pick a time that is convenient for both of you—not when your daughter's children are due home from school, or your son's car just blew the engine. The place for your talk is important, too. You need to be able to see and touch each other physically. But if you are separated by miles, the telephone is better than not talking at all. If possible, meet in one of your homes early in the day when neither of you is too tired. You'll feel free to cry, raise your voices, and then embrace. A public place should be avoided so that both of you can respond freely.

Stick to the subject. Don't get off on side issues that happened umpteen years ago. You're hurt now.

You love your child. You want to do whatever is necessary to build and nurture your friendship.

Be sure your adult kid knows what it is you're saying. Ask, "Was I clear? Do you understand what I mean?" If she doesn't, go over the same subject again. She may not agree with you, but that isn't the problem; you just want to discuss your feelings and what it is you see to be the main issue. State your position without trying to lay a guilt trip. Guilt erects walls that must be toppled by love and understanding. Try to look at the problem from her perspective and understand why you disagree. Only then can you come to a mutual respect.

You may need to lift your heart to God for wisdom and patience many times throughout your conversation. Remember that His help is immediate and His presence will draw you together. "For where two or three come together in my name, there am I with them." (Matthew 18:20)

Let's be realistic though. You are you, and I am me. As individuals, we will never totally understand each other whether we are relating with our children, our parents, our mates, or our friends. As Mortimer J. Adler writes in his book, *How To Speak/How To Listen,* "We can never completely get out of ourselves and into the other person's shoes and see things as he or she sees them."

It may be that our communication patterns and selective listening are long-established habits—habits which began years ago when we stopped talking and listening to each other. It may take some time for us to remove old barriers and to build a trust that lets the other inside. It was Mark Twain who made the observation that, "A habit cannot be tossed out the window; it must be coaxed down the stairs a step at a time."

ATTENTION!

I've heard wives say, and have even said it myself, "My husband doesn't talk to me." That may be true, but it might be more accurate to say, "My husband doesn't listen to me." His eyes are glazed as I tell him about my conversation with a neighbor. He glances back at his book when I pause before going to the next subject. He yawns instead of responding to my question. All of these tell me that he hasn't really heard what I'm saying. Have I picked the wrong time to talk to him? Is that why he doesn't listen? But, then, do I listen when he talks? Really listen? Am I truly interested in what he has to say?

As a general rule, we aren't good listeners. We don't even listen to ourselves. We're either occupied with what we will say next or when we can get back to what we were doing or reading before being interrupted. Listening takes more effort than talking. We can run off at the mouth, spouting "cheap talk" without a thought. The words just pour out. But to listen attentively, we have to concentrate on the words we hear and then interpret them to our understanding. That's hard work. But like love and forgiveness, we must bring our will into action and determine to listen.

Of course, we have to screen what we hear.

Throughout the course of a day we hear TV commercials, children playing outside, loud music from passing cars, and obscenities on the street. If we listened attentively to all these noises, we'd go crazy. But has it become a habit to turn off what we don't like to hear from our grown-up kids as well?

Just as we learn other skills, we can learn to listen, and we can learn to talk. It may take a few trial runs, but to really communicate with our grown-up kids makes the effort worthwhile. Maybe we need to ask ourselves why it is so hard to listen. Could it be because we don't want to hear something that may hurt us? or stir up unpleasant feelings? or have to make a change in our lives?

Yes.

No.

All of the above.

I've found that those people who seem most adept at listening to others are the same ones who have learned to listen to God. And how can you tell if a person listens to God? Because that person accepts criticism and admonition from others as from God, and is willing to change and grow. He also spends time reading God's Word and applying it to his life. He is not only a hearer of the Word, but also a doer (James 1:22).

This is what I want to learn to do: not just glance at the words in the Bible, but listen to what God is saying to me, and then do it. As I become more sensitive to God's voice, I'll also learn to listen better to my grown-up kids, to my husband, to my parents, to my friends, and to my relatives. I will become a "communicator" in the real sense of the word.

Ideally I want to be like Samuel who said, "Speak, for your servant is listening" (I Samuel 3:10). But before Samuel said that, he had listened to the advice of Eli, another human being. Samuel was being prepared to become the go-between for the people of Israel and the Lord. He was both a listener and a speaker. He was a humble man who was willing to change and be changed. We need the same kind of spirit if we want to touch not only our children but also our God.

FOR DISCUSSION AND ENCOURAGEMENT

- Has God used someone, perhaps an adult child, to call attention to your faults and failures? How did you respond?
- Are you as sensitive to others' feelings as you are to your own?
- Even though it's impossible to totally understand another person, try to see life through the eyes of your grown-up child. Write down some of the insights and different viewpoints that come through this exercise.
- Try being a listener before talking. Really hear what your child is saying. Ask, "Are you saying? . . ." Be sure you understand before replying.
- Spend a quiet time alone with God—just listening. Don't talk at him; let Him do

the talking. Thank Him for showing you the good, as well as the hard, things that you've been avoiding.

- Get together with your grown-up kid for the primary purpose of communicating at a deep level. It may be the best time you've had in ages.

- A good book on a biblical approach to interpersonal communication is, *The Trauma of Transparency* by J. Grant Howard. Try it; you'll like it! You might also try *The Friendship Factor* by Alan Loy McGinnis.

By wisdom a house is built, and through understanding it is established; through knowledge its rooms are filled with rare and beautiful treasures.—Proverbs 24:3-4

11

Yours, Mine, and Ours

We've been talking about the joys and jolts of relating with our grown-up kids. Suppose you had not only yours, but also his—and ours?

"Oh what tangled webs we weave," said a mother of a "Yours/Mine/Ours" family. Natalie has five children from a previous marriage; her husband George has two, and they share a lovely daughter. And I thought I was confused!

I talked to this couple about their relationships with each other as well as several other couples.

Delores and Marv are a "Yours" family. When Delores married Marv, he had two children from a previous marriage. She had none.

Claire and Jack are a "Mine" family married later in life. They are much the same as the previous couple, except Claire brought her grown-up married daughter into the marriage. Jack had no children.

Harriette and Bill are a "Yours/Ours" family. Bill had two children from a previous marriage. Together they had two more.

Betty and Wayne are a "Yours/Mine" family. They set up housekeeping with her boy and girl and his son.

All of these mixed relationships may seem confusing, and I'm sure they are; but I believe the insights the different couples shared will be of help to those who make up a growing segment of family life in America: the divorced and remarried.

What kind of family is yours? Maybe you can find some answers—at least some hope—as you hear what these parents have to say.

YOURS

When Delores married Marv, he had two small children to raise. Their mother had left the state and given all custody to Marv. He was relieved that his children would now have a mother, but Delores had misgivings. Oh, not about the children. She already loved them. Not able to bear children herself, she was delighted for the opportunity to be a mother. But would Marv accept her strong views on discipline? Could he give her the freedom she needed to raise his children her way?

An organized and thoughtful woman, Delores insisted they discuss the problems and pitfalls before the wedding. What goals did they each have for family life? Where did they agree? How did they differ? Their first discussion ended with tears and angry words, so they decided to let some time go by before setting a wedding date. Several weeks passed before they came up with mutually agreeable rules. Knowing those rules would change as the children, Timmy and Tina grew, Delores and Marv also talked about their views on raising teenagers. Finally, they discovered ways they could both compromise, and determined to back each other up—regardless— when it came to disciplining these already out-of-control children.

Although Delores felt and behaved as though she were the natural mother, almost from the beginning she heard words like, "You wouldn't do that if you were their real mother!" "How can you understand? You never had children of your own !"

Even the children picked up on the idea of a "wicked stepmother," and Delores had to pray daily for strength to continue her loving care without a heavy burden of guilt. Regarding her relationship with the children, she said, "I knew that if we had smooth sailing, people would say, 'Well, since they're not yours, you can afford to be lenient.' And if our relationship suffered, I would be accused of not doing a good job. I think a lot of misplaced guilt is laid at the door of a stepparent!"

Many times, when his son balked at Delores's discipline with the words, "You're not my mother," Marv had to intervene. This happened often between Tim and Delores, and she still grieves that her relationship with him was never as close as she wished. However, Tina did respond to Delores's love and discipline, and they have remained good friends.

Those growing-up years were hard on all of them, but this couple decided to hang tough. And today Delores has some words of advice to those "wicked stepmothers" trying to raise a family.

1. Don't rush into marriage. An ounce of prevention could be the best medicine when children are concerned. Talk. Set rules. Straighten out your goals before you say, "I do." "And though it may sound mercenary," Delores added, "talk over the inheritance and how it will affect the wife."

2. Don't allow the children to play father against mother. The natural parent must take over in these situations. "Yes, she is your mother in this home! You will obey her."

3. Don't be afraid to discipline your stepchildren any more than you would your own. God's Word teaches us that if we love our children, we will discipline and train them (Proverbs 13:24).

4. Don't hesitate to ask advice from a respected friend or minister. No one has all the answers to raising a family. Just being the natural parent doesn't necessarily provide wisdom!

5. Don't come between the child and his natural parent. Never talk against them. This goes for any mother and father, I think. Why chip away at the foundation? It will weaken the entire structure. Delores said that she often stayed home alone for a week at a time so Marv could develop a strong bond with Tim.

This "Yours" family continues to grow in their

relationships. As grown-up kids, Tim and Tina are still very important to both Delores and Marv. When I asked Delores how she feels about Tim's new baby boy, she answered, "I still feel left out of Tim's life. He has never allowed me to be close to him, and though I love that baby with all my heart, I feel a separation, a sense of not belonging."

Tim has never been willing to meet Delores even half way, but she no longer questions, "Is there anything else I should do?" She has committed the situation to God and is at peace. Who knows what the future holds? With God nothing is impossible.

How about Tina? Recently she told her step-mother. "Mom, I don't know how you stood us kids. We were really a handful. But I thank you for loving us. I really appreciate all you've done. I love you!"

Delores and Marv's "Yours" family has had its share of thorns on a rose-strewn path, but at this point in time, Tina is close to the family; Tim is mellowing some and drawing closer, and Delores and Marv have a great relationship. They look forward to retirement with expectancy and excitement. The past years have developed their endurance and, also, their love.

MINE

Claire and Jack's "Mine" family may at first glance seem similar to Delores and Marv's, but Claire married Jack after her daughter was grown. There was no problem of discipline or having to deal with a stepchild. However, Claire's daughter resented Jack, and he felt it.

Whenever Claire and her daughter Jan got together, they totally absorbed themselves in each other, leaving Jack out of the conversations. At times Claire even asked him to leave the room. This kind of behavior, instead of drawing the family closer, built walls.

Jack became noisy and anxious; Claire was over-protective with her daughter; and Jan made excuses not to be with her mother and stepfather.

Not only was the immediate family affected, but the grandchildren's relationship with their grand-father suffered. Claire has faced this and recently admitted, "I believe it has been my attitude that separated Jack from the rest of the family." She said she felt Jan and the grandchildren were hers and not really Jack's. Her possessiveness had been a major cause of the misunderstandings in the family.

But an unexpected heart attack changed all of that.

When Claire spent a month in an out-of-town hospital going through tests and ultimately open-heart surgery, Jack discovered that Claire's family was really *his* after all.

Long trips together every morning and evening brought Jan and her stepfather into a relationship that spanned any previous misconceptions. After one particularly trying day, he broke down and cried, "All these years, I thought that if your mother died, I would be forgotten because I'm not really your father. But now I know that you and the kids love me. You love me for myself."

Jan put aside all her resentments and pride and

willingly accepted Jack into her heart—and her family.

All "Mine" families do not take such turns. But if you have grown-up kids and your husband or wife has none, do all in your power to include your mate in the family circle.

How?

1. Let your adult children know that you still love them, but that now your first concern is for your new partner. They must learn to accept him or her in all the family functions. "Love me, love my darlin'."

2. Don't push your mate at the grandchildren. Let him win their love his own way. You love him. Why shouldn't they?

3. Don't leave your spouse out of family discussions and problems. Give your spouse the joys of sharing parenthood and grandparenthood. It will do wonders for a drooping self-esteem, and it will even make your marriage a better one.

> *All the believers were one in heart and mind. No one claimed that any of his possessions was his own, but they shared everything they had. (Acts 4:32)*

Even their children?

YOURS/OURS

It was a second marriage for both Harriette and Bill. Though Harriette brought no children into the marriage, Bill had a fourteen-year-old son and a five-year-old daughter who lived most of the time with their mother and part of the time with him.

The marriage barely survived the problem teenager who used drugs and refused to cooperate with Harriette. Bill said, "You'll just have to go along with this as long as the kids are with me."

But the rough ways Bill spoke to Patrick and the way he bent over backwards to "show the kids I love them," created more problems. He gave presents instead of parental discipline, almost ignoring the wife who wanted so much to be a part of the family. Then three years later, their first child was born.

Now Patrick was the jealous one. And as he grew taller and began to hover over his stepmother, she turned all her attention and love to the new baby. It looked like a no-win situation.

Tension lifted when Bill was free of child support. Harriette no longer felt resentment that his kids had more material benefits than theirs. Even the children began to warm up to their stepmother and the now two small children in the family. Harriet said, "Patrick and Dawn really loved the little ones. There was no sibling rivalry because of the age difference." She sighed and a smile lit her face. "I'm so thankful we got through those trying years intact. The relationship with Patrick is not entirely healed yet, but I'm praying. And as for Dawn, she looked to me as her mother, and I love it."

When I asked Harriette if a good relationship with Bill's grown-up kids was important to her, she replied, "Oh, yes, but not just because they're his kids. I like them as friends." She laughed. "I admit,

I didn't like them when they were young, but I really do now."

How about the younger children? They both told me that Patrick and Dawn are their brother and sister. They feel no different toward them than toward each other.

Harriette and Bill admit to making mistakes, who doesn't? But they agree with Delores and Marv's suggestions. Talk over the child/stepparent problems before marriage. Keep talking. Keep loving. They also added:

1. In a "Yours/Ours" family, don't even think "yours" or "mine." Think ours. Children are a gift from God, and happy are those who have many (Psalm 127:3-5).

2. Never put each other down in the presence of your children. Show a united front. Children need that kind of emotional—and physical—support.

God gave us good rules for Christian households:

> *Wives, submit to your husbands, as is fitting in the Lord. Husbands, love your wives and do not be harsh with them. Children, obey your parents in everything, for this pleases the Lord. Fathers, do not embitter your children, or they will become discouraged.*
> *(Colossians 3:18-21)*

YOURS/MINE

When Betty and Wayne got together, they began their life with her two small children and his teenaged son.

All seemed to go well at first. Betty was not only

able to hold down a well-paying job, but she had a built-in babysitter. As soon as Evan got home from high school, he was to pick up the children from nursery school, clean house and start dinner. He didn't seem to mind. At least not until he reached his senior year. Then he wanted time to participate in school clubs and sports. His friends laughed when he told them, "I have to clean the living room and go to the grocery store."

Wayne also began to resent Betty's demanding expectations of his son. He argued, "The boy should have more time to himself." But she had a ready answer. "How can we make the payments on this house if I have to put out money on a baby-sitter?"

So the strained relations grew.

Betty and Wayne's marriage had been rocky from the beginning. Not a strong Christian, Betty seemed unable to draw on God's wisdom and only put more pressure on Evan. Her struggle between guilt and trying to make a living broke through several times when she took her children and moved out. But she loved Wayne, and in only a few days, she would come home, this time vowing to make it work.

Wayne, trying to compensate and also trying to save the marriage began to put more pressure on his son, too. Evan had no life of his own, and his resentment grew not only against his father and stepmother but also toward his stepbrother and sister.

Always being in the middle of every family fight, Evan finally moved out of the house. Now as a grown-up kid, he is estranged from Betty and

Wayne. The two small children have lost their big brother, and there is still much pain in this home.

But God. . . .

These words to the nation of Israel could well be applied to Betty and Wayne's home. In fact, any one of us may heed God's voice and count on His promise.

> *. . . if my people, who are called by my name, will humble themselves and pray and seek my face and turn from their wicked ways, then will I hear from heaven and will forgive their sin and will heal their land." (II Chronicles 7:14)*

The relationship between Betty, Wayne and Evan is not yet healed. All parties still hurt too much to reach out to each other, so they have no words of encouragement or advice to others in their predicament. But read on. Natalie and George end this chapter on a positive note.

Yours/Mine/Ours

I left the biggest and the best for last because Natalie and George have put it all together and have one of the most satisfying relationships with their grown-up kids that I've ever seen.

When I asked them if having close ties with their grown-up kids was important, they both nodded and emphatically answered, "Yes, very!" They have seven grown-up children, and one almost grown teenager. Five are hers from a previous marriage, two are his, and the youngest one is theirs. Yours,

Mine, and Ours. But Natalie and George look upon all these children as "ours." They always have.

When they married, both were dedicated Christians. Together, their goal for themselves and for their children was to make Christ the center of their home. Here are some of the ways they accomplished it.

In the beginning, they found themselves as weekend parents to each others' children. "His" lived the rest of the week with their mother and stepfather. One of "hers" lived with his father and stepmother. George made every effort to treat her children as his own, being especially careful not to show favoritism to either set of kids. They had family discussion times in which they expressed their feelings. "Our love to each of you is equal," George said. "There may be times when you don't believe this because of a disciplinary problem or some other special circumstance. But it's true. There are no favorites in this family."

Natalie accepted George's leadership as father in the home, and though she sometimes resented his discipline, she supported his decisions. At least outwardly. In the course of our interview, she said many times, "If Christ had not been the Lord of our home, we would not have made it." She is confident that Christ molded them into a family in spite of the difficulties, and there were many. Today, as yesterday, they are a unit.

She laughed as she remembered a comment made by "their" youngest daughter one evening after a busy day with all the stepchildren. "Mom, when are you gonna get divorced so I can have a stepdad, too?" It seems this child felt strangely alone and different because she didn't have a step-parent like her brothers and sisters.

Now, all but that last daughter are grown-up kids. Natalie and George enjoy the companionship of each one who drops in, and their home is often filled with laughing grown-ups and their wives, husbands and friends. They, too, have given some suggestions for a good relationship with those adult children.

1. Accept stepchildren into the family with the same responsibility as those who are born of both parents.

2. Teach the children by your actions that prayer plus faith equal freedom. Freedom to love. Freedom to grow.

3. When there is jealousy and anger, don't shove it down with resentment. Learn to deal with your emotions honestly.

4. Natalie added a thought she once read and now applies to the grown-up kids who have chosen to follow their own lifestyles. Don't push. Don't pull. Walk beside those adult children.

Yours. Mine. Ours. If your family fits into any of these categories, you are one of many. It won't be easy to establish lasting, loving relationships with every child, but it can happen. The effort you make, along with your confidence in a living, all-powerful God, will give your family strength and stability.

FOR DISCUSSION AND ENCOURAGEMENT

- Reread the suggestions given by these real-life families. They not only apply to stepfamilies but also speak to any mom and dad truly desirous of a strong bond with their children.

- Remember that good advice: Don't push. They'll only dig their heels in deeper. Wouldn't you? Don't pull. A tug-of-war means someone loses. Walk beside your grown-up kids. As parents and children grow in wisdom and stature, you'll be surprised to find how often you see eye to eye.

Now to him who is able to do immeasurably more than all we ask or imagine, according to his power that is at work within us, to him be glory in the church and in Christ Jesus throughout all generations, for ever and ever! Amen.—Ephesians 3:20-21

12

Great
Expectations

MANY YEARS AGO MY favorite aunt offered me five words of advice, words from the Bible that echoed through my head as I faced one trial after another in bringing up six children. A theologian may argue that the words were taken out of context; yet they fit so well within the context of my life, I want to share them with you.

"And it came to pass. . . ."

That's it?

Yes.

These five words are repeated over and over again in the King James Version of the gospels. On the surface, that phrase is purely introductory; but to the believer, they can be words of hope and expectation.

Think about it. The late-night feedings came to pass. The bout with measles came to pass. The surgery and recovery came to pass. The rebellion and long hair came to pass. The alcohol treatment program came to pass. The misunderstandings, the heartaches, the pain of rejection and loss came to pass. At the time of testing, we feel certain there is no end to our trouble, but:

". . . And it came to pass."

I can't say how often the remembrance of these words and the truth they convey helped me persevere under pressure. Of course, that uphill climb over the "pass" sometimes leaves us so breathless and weary that no words or truth penetrates our grief.

Matt and Bonnie are in that place right now with their grown-up kids. Once on the mission field, this couple was, through circumstances, forced to return to America and to a culture foreign to their sensitive teenagers. A few years in a fast-paced, urban high school changed the lives of their two children. The daughter, a beautiful, talented girl, succumbed to peer pressure and is now pregnant. She is unmarried, unrepentant and unmanageable. Their son turned to drugs. Neither of these children, now in their early twenties, makes enough money to be self-supporting, so both continue to occupy rooms in the family home.

How are the parents coping? Bonnie has taken a job in a department store, and Matt spends as much time away from home as possible. Their hearts still yearn to serve God, yet they punish themselves with guilt. "What did we do wrong?" "How can God use us in His service when our own children have made such a mess of their lives?"

Matt's eyes are dulled with desperation. He admits he doesn't know what to do. He loves his daughter and is relieved she decided to have the baby instead of an abortion. He also loves his son and prays that the resolve to "stay clean" is genuine . . . this time. He and Bonnie agree that they don't want to send their grown-up children away to face difficult and uncertain futures alone. At least at home, they can keep an eye on them.

What would you do? Do you have an answer for this suffering family?

"And it came to pass. . . ."

Those five words sound trite at this point in Matt and Bonnie's lives, but the worry and disappointment will pass. A year from now, they will look back on these days and thank God for His loving grace. I know because I have done that.

It has been one year since I decided to write this book; and a year and a half has passed since those hours I sat in counselling sessions at "New Beginnings." We, and our children, are one year further along in our growth and in our love and concern for each other. Maybe you'd like to know where we are now compared to where we were when this book began.

The son who went through the alcohol and drug rehabilitation program has become the loving, caring person he was meant to be. No longer sullen and angry, he often drops by the house to talk, to share his life, to voice his concerns. He's not perfect. We don't expect him to be. He's also had a couple of setbacks, but each time he stopped and said to himself, "Hey, what am I doing? I don't ever want to become what I was." It's been months since he has put chemicals into his body. He actively pursues a sport, dresses in clean, fashionable clothes, and has even managed to move out of a rented apartment into his first home. The Lord is patiently guiding him into *His* perfect will. He even comes to church now and then. Not because we ask. We don't. He comes because he wants to . . . because the Lord's love is so strong and tender.

The daughter who was out of work a year ago found not one but two jobs she loves, and she is now contemplating the mission field.

Our other son and his wife had a safe sailing trip to Mexico; two daughters have had babies; and the last daughter moved out of her room a month ago and is adapting to university dorm life several hundred miles away.

We've had worries this past year: storms and seasickness; a baby rushed in an ambulance to an Intensive Care Unit fifty miles away; disappointments; and disagreements. But each and every event came to pass, and in its passing we came through more finely tuned.

Remember Alice and Sara? Both of those mothers have seen their daughters step out to take control of their own lives. Alice's daughter is now married and living in another state. Sara's daughter is holding down a responsible job. She paid off her bills, apologized to her parents for causing so much trouble, and is growing up. Most, although not all, of the grown-up kids I wrote about have faced their own mistakes and are making them right. Some never will. Maybe your child is one of those who refuses to grow up. You're disappointed. You're discouraged.

Don't be.

Take these five words, "And it came to pass . . ." as your own; and as you trust God through the circumstances, He will teach you to rise above them and to put your feelings about your grown-up kids into proper perspective.

GREAT EXPECTATIONS OR WILLING ACCEPTANCE?

Often the parents who suffer the greatest disappointments are those with the greatest expectations for their children. We hold that newborn son in our arms and see him graduating with the highest honors: not behind bars for drunken driving. We dress our infant daughter in pink ruffles and imagine her walking down the aisle in clouds of white chiffon: not standing in line for a welfare check. We want, for our children, not only what we have but much, much more. We long for them to enjoy a sense of self-esteem, the respect of their peers, and a growing fellowship with God. Our expectations are good and right. But they are not always fulfilled.

Here come some more hard words.

Our children do not always turn out as we hope they will. They may not choose our lifestyles, our goals or our faith in God. If that happens, we are disappointed in them, in ourselves, and, all too often, we blame God. What happened to Proverbs

22:6? "Train a child in the way he should go, and when he is old he will not turn from it."

Doesn't that mean that if we do our part as a loving, faithful Christian parent, our kids will turn out right? they will follow Christ and make us proud? Many take it as a guarantee, and we think either we failed as parents or God let us down. He promised, and He didn't come through.

Not so. Read the verse again. Does it say, "You be a good Christian parent, and your child will grow up to be a good Christian, too"?

No. The verse in Proverbs is one of a group of sayings written to help parents discipline and control their children. But the children also have a responsibility to learn from our example. If, as adults, they choose to depart from our training, they must answer for their own decisions.

We do our best to follow God's directions in training our children, but then we must also follow His other guidelines: *"Do not be anxious about anything"* (Philippians 4:6); *"Do not fret because of evil men"* (Psalm 37:1); and we know that our children must *"Believe in the Lord Jesus"* (Acts 16:31) for themselves. We cannot believe for them. We cannot convince, coerce, or cajole them to the Savior. But we can be calm, serene, and full of faith.

How? By willing acceptance of God's purpose in *our* lives.

It is trying to hold on to our grown-up kids, or to *our* dreams of what we think they should be, that turns disappointment into torment. And torment results when we refuse to give up the idols of our hearts. We can all expect a certain amount of pain and anguish, but torment in the life of a believer is not God's will. Torment eats away at our insides; it drains our energy and zest for life. Torment, the opposite of peace and serenity, is unnecessary when we willingly accept God's will and His right to give us whatever He has chosen for us. A turn-of-the-century clergyman, John Hill Aughey, said, "God brings men into deep waters, not to drown them, but to cleanse them."

By all means hold on to your great expectations. For your children, and for yourself. Keep dreaming. Keep praying. Your grown-up children can be, and often are, the best friends you'll ever have. At the same time, let go of your disappointments. Willingly accept God's plan for your life. Someone has said, "Adversity introduces a man to himself." Do you know who you are yet? Have you discovered if you are a winner or a whiner? A praiser or a pouter? By the time our kids are grown-up, we should be, too.

MATURE BONDS

If our dreams are all tied up in our children, we'll be in knots. Only God can unravel our tangled hopes and expectations and weave our remaining days into a colorful design.

Our remaining days? What a somber thought! But the fact that we have grown-up kids ought to be evidence that we have lived quite a few years. It's time we faced the fact that we probably have more of a past than a future. We can determine to enjoy what's left.

Velma decided after Cliff died that she wanted to use some of the insurance money for a trip to Europe. The media painted a grim picture of hijackings, air disasters, and revolutionary coups. Velma's grown-up children objected to her plan.

"It's not safe, Mom."

"Dad wouldn't have wanted you to go."

"You should save the money."

Translation:

"Now that you don't have to take care of Dad, you can take care of our kids."

"You're too old to take care of yourself."

"What business does a sixty-year-old woman have jetting around the world?"

"If you spend the money, we won't get it when you're gone."

Velma only smiled and shook her head. She made reservations, contacted an old friend, joined up with a tour group, and fulfilled her own dream to walk the streets of Paris and ride the double-decker buses of London.

When she returned a month later, not only did she have a new image of herself, her children also saw her in a different light. Velma did not allow her grown-up kids to dissuade her anymore than she would have allowed a friend to talk her out of her dream. If she had stayed home to care for the grandchildren instead of flying away, she would have been resentful or worse yet, a martyr. She has made her own happiness and shaped a new future without a husband; and, although her children may not yet realize it, she has given them a sense of freedom, too. Their mom can make decisions on her own. She has a life that is separate from theirs.

Velma told me last week that she is planning another trip, this time to China. Velma's bonds with her children have matured, and she's enjoying them and herself more.

Now that your children are grown, what do you want to do? What does your partner want? Have the two of you always wanted to travel? Has it been a secret desire to have a swimming pool in your backyard? Do you both enjoy caring for the grandchildren now and then? Would you rather not?

Talk over your future with each other. Let your grown-up kids know that you're not tired of them— you're just tired. You need to get away. You want to renew your relationship and get re-acquainted with who you are. You deserve some time alone.

My husband and I have been married over thirty-six years. Our oldest son will be thirty-five soon. Our youngest daughter just moved out for her first year at college. For the first time in thirty-five years, we are alone. Though we have been together for almost four decades, there was only one and a half years that we weren't primarily occupied with the needs of our family. We're getting reacquainted. We're falling in love all over again. We really like each other. It's great! We have plans to go to the mountains next weekend and to the coast a couple of weeks after that. We're comfortable reading quietly in the same room or pursuing our hobbies in different rooms.

Our grown-up kids smile and whisper, "Look at Mom and Dad. Aren't they cute?" I hear them. I see them watching us, observing what they will one day be.

We're going to grow old together. We're going to grow together. We'll keep learning and growing as long as we have breath. And we'll love and rejoice over our grown-up kids and maybe even their grown-up kids. This business of parenting has its rewards. Mature bonds.

Arthur Schopenhauer, a German philosopher of the early 1800s, commented, "The first forty years of life give us the text; the next thirty supply the commentary on it."

FOR DISCUSSION AND ENCOURAGEMENT

- The Bible tells us that children are a reward from the Lord. List at least four ways your children have made your life fuller and more satisfying. Then turn it around. List four ways you have made your parents' lives fuller and more satisfying.

- How do you feel about your grown-up kids? Are they your friends? Or do you feel you must be in control? Do you tend to demand more from them than you would any other "best" friend?

- Have you set yourself up as "Supermom and/or Superdad"? Are you trying to win a popularity contest with your grandchildren?

- Remember that "Serenity Prayer"? Take it apart, phrase by phrase; then make it your own.

GOD—When we pray to God, we must recognize His sovereignty, His Lordship over every detail of our personal existence. He is in control. He is never surprised or caught off guard by our circumstances. He is God.

GRANT ME—We are incapable of fulfilling our own deepest needs, and we must learn to come immediately to our heavenly Father with our requests. In Philippians 4:6 we are instructed to pray with thanksgiving. Perhaps the reason we have had so many unanswered prayers is that we have left out an important ingredient. Prayer without thanksgiving is like a hot fudge sundae without the fudge.

THE SERENITY—To be calm and cheerful in the midst of turmoil is the essence of maturity. How does it happen?

TO ACCEPT THE THINGS I CANNOT CHANGE—When I worry about those things that are out of my control, I get off balance. When I try to fix situations and mold people into my ideas of how they should be, I attempt to fill God's shoes. Willing acceptance of those things I cannot change is the first step to maturity.

COURAGE—"The ability to control fear when facing danger or pain." Cicero wrote, "A man of courage is also full of faith." It takes faith in an all-sufficient

God to put aside fear and face danger or pain. Have you received Jesus Christ as your own personal Savior and Lord? If not, why not bow your head right now and invite the Son of God, who bore your penalty for sin, into your life?

Yet to all who received him, to those who believed in his name, he gave the right to become children of God. (John 1:12)

TO CHANGE THE THINGS I CAN—I don't have to remain ignorant, or bitter, or dirty. I can study, forgive, or take a shower. I cannot change the basic shape of my body, but I can get rid of some of the extra pounds. It takes courage to make changes. Most of us fear change especially when it comes to relationships with family and friends. Take the initiative. Say, "I'm sorry." Be courageous. Say, "No, not today."

AND WISDOM TO KNOW THE DIFFERENCE—Oh, it does take wisdom to know whether to accept circumstances or to change them; and God has promised that our prayer for wisdom will be answered. James wrote:

If any of you lacks wisdom, he should ask God, who gives generously to all without finding fault, and it will be given to him. (James 1:5)

He then adds that our asking must be in faith. It's humbling to ask God for wisdom. We like to think we have the answers. We want others to see us as all-knowing, intelligent adults. But as Charles Spurgeon said, "The doorstep to the temple of wisdom is a knowledge of our own ignorance."

- Have Great Expectations for your grown-up kids.
- Have Great Expectations for yourself.
- We have a great God.

Epilogue

ONCE AGAIN OUR FAMILY sat around a room, our eyes and hearts reaching out to that same troubled son, our third child. He had come far since the years of overcoming his addictions; he was a real-estate broker and the owner of several rental properties. He was about to celebrate his second wedding anniversary after having waited thirty-four years for the "girl of his dreams."

Four months ago we gathered around their newborn son, Matthew Earl, to rejoice over the birth of the first grandson to carry on the family name. Our rejoicing has now turned to sorrow, for Matthew, our precious baby, has returned to his Heavenly Father, a victim of SIDS (Sudden Infant Death Syndrome).

My husband and I were three thousand miles

from home when our son called in the middle of the night with the shocking news that his baby—our grandson—was dead. A daughter called and assured us that every brother and sister was on the way to the hospital and would be upholding the bereaved parents. The pastor, too, had been called and would be standing by.

The flight back across the United States and the drive home from the airport seemed like an eternity, but we were soon welcomed into our home and into the arms of our grown children.

As my tear-filled eyes rested on each of my children, I thought, "These are not grown-up kids. These are grown-up kids. They are adults with grown-up problems: They are acting with maturity and honor; teaching me how to be vulnerable and open with my grief; and helping me learn how to receive words of comfort and instruction.

As those difficult days have evolved into weeks, I'm more able to be objective, to see God's loving care, and to know there is a future for my despairing son and his precious wife. God's Son is still shining behind those dark clouds that brought such a chill to our lives.

I wanted this last word with you, dear parents of Grown-Up Kids, to underline all that has been discussed before in this short book: Build those relationships; listen to your children without judgment; teach them by your example that Jesus Christ is alive—that His Word is truth.

Don't give up if or when your adult children seem to walk away from the Lord. You may be confident of this very thing—". . . He who began a good work in you [and in your children] will perfect it until the day of Christ Jesus" (Philippians 1:6).

My grown-up children still need my husband and me when they suffer, and although we can no longer kiss their hurts to make them well, we can sit with them, hold their hands, and point them to our Heavenly Father. All of us, whatever our age, are still Grown-Up Kids. We need our Father's comfort and love—and so do you!

As I close the pages of this book, I join Paul's voice as he speaks, "Blessed be the God and Father of our Lord Jesus Christ, the Father of mercies and God of all comfort; who comforts us in all our affliction so that we may be able to comfort those who are in any affliction with the comfort with which we are comforted by God" (2 Corinthians 1:3-4).